Carpe Diem,

STAYING
RELEVANT

240-508-2169 cell

LIFE IS GREAT
Publishing

STAYING RELEVANT

Before, During, and After Retirement

DEMETRIUS FELDER

Staying Relevant
Before, During, and After Retirement
Copyright 2018 by Demetrius Felder

For information contact: Holisticplanners.com

Book cover design by Bemnet Yemesgen
Book design by Bluebobo

Library of Congress Cataloging-in-Publication Data
Felder,Demetrius.

Staying Relevant: Before,During, and After Retirement/Demetrius Felder 2017915182

ISBN: 978-0-9990042-5-8
First Edition: January 2018

Dedication

For Zander and Langston, the reason I inhale and exhale.
Leaders, warriors, physically strong, mentally stronger,
millionaires, billionaires, world changers, entrepreneurs.
You will always be more than enough.

Sterling Ashby thanks for teaching me that character,
strength, and faith are never revealed in good times or
through words but only in your darkest moments and
through your actions. Because of your character, strength,
and faith, your legacy will live forever.
I will forever step into the big question because of you.

Contents

Biblically Backed

"Within the covers of the Bible are the answers for all the problems men face."
— Ronald Reagan

CHAPTER	VERSUS
Introduction	Proverbs 4:2, Deuteronomy 32:2, Deuteronomy 8:18, John 10:10
Armed and Dangerous	Matthew 7:15, 1 John 4:1
Self-Talk and Self Sabotage	Romans 9:20, Proverbs 4:23
Look in the Mirror	John 8:32, James 1:23
Neurofinance	Romans 8:5-6, Romans 12:2
Project Xero	Romans 13:8, Proverbs 22:26
Investment Strategies by Age and Stage	Ecclesiastes 11
Relationship Karma	Proverbs 31:10-31
Life Goes On	Psalm 86:5

Courgaronomics	Proverbs 31:10-31
Viagraville	1 Corinthians 10:13, Mark 14:38, 1 Timothy 6:9
Casino Capitalism	1 Timothy 6:10
Ready or Not	2 Corinthians 5:17
Roadblocks to Retirement	Proverbs 12:11, 1 Samuel 8
New Age Retirement	Genesis 2:2
Sudden Wealth	Malachi 3:10, Deuteronomy 8:17, 1 Samuel 2:7
Escaping the Middle Class	Proverbs 4:7
Cost of Aging Gracefully	Matthew 25:21
Long Term Care	1 Timothy 5, Leviticus 19:3
A-Bomb	Hebrews 11
Conversations That Matter	Proverbs 13:22
Health the New Wealth	Ecclesiastes 7-12
Skill Monetization	Matthew 25:14–30
Conclusion	1 Corinthians 9:24
Worksheets	Isaiah 28:29

Spiritual mentor:

Stephen Chandler | Senior Pastor www.destinyharvest.tv

Introduction

Life is short. Legacy is forever.

You hear it all the time: I'll be working until I keel over." "There's no such thing as retirement anymore." "Retirement is just waiting to die." As a financial advisor I've heard these panicked statements numerous times, and in many ways, the negativity they project is true—if you follow the traditional route toward retirement.

This book is a product of speaking with numerous clients, friends, and strangers. I've found that whether I talked to a person who has been successful in life and money, or to someone struggling with finances, having a fulfilling retirement with purpose and opportunities for growth – a retirement that allows them to stay relevant – is their wish.

I also listened to a lot of people who were concerned about money. Typically, these people just didn't know how to start or what to do. These conversations inspired me to explain the basics to the most sophisticated retirement strategies as well as new ways to preserve

1

and protect your life savings. As you read, be ready to be challenged and to think differently about retirement and money because I wrote this book like the bible as a resource for all phases of life. You can have great comfort in knowing that just like the bible you can read it cover to cover or only one chapter, but it will provide you everything you need at the perfect moment.

Beyond the facts and figures, *Staying Relevant* takes a look at cutting edge science, which has begun to tell us how the brain's wiring is critical to understanding financial decisions.

Now that I have set the stage for your journey through this book, you have a decision to make. You can purchase this book (If you have already, thank you.) or you can simply walk away. If you are still on the fence, take a look at the table of contents. As you will see, this book is not made for just one read; it is a book you will return to again and again at different stages in your life.

Use *Staying Relevant* as a roadmap. Enjoy the journey.
Carpe Diem,

Demetrius Felder

How to Read this Book

"It is the mark of an educated mind to be able to entertain a thought without accepting it."
— Aristotle

Get ready for a new way to approach retirement. I believe in my heart you will achieve your goals if you apply what you will learn in this book and strive to become the best version of you.

Information is the key to making changes. I hope you have the vision and see the opportunity in the ways the information in *Staying Relevant* can positively help you have a fulfilling retirement with purpose and opportunities for growth - to stay relevant before, during, and after retirement. But the real question, which I cannot answer, is that upon completion of this book, will YOU apply this new information IMMEDIATELY by completing the worksheets and leveraging the resources provided. If you do, you will succeed in your quest for relevance, significance, and meaning.

I want to make sure that the time you spend with this book is time well spent, so I've invested countless hours writing and rewriting to make sure this book provides value to readers. I did not try to wow you with large words or financial jargon, but instead wrote in common language and plain English. This book is broken down by life stages and life events. It includes simple steps to help you reach your goal. It includes nontraditional and traditional methods — methods the big Wall Street firms, insurance companies, and large mutual fund companies do not want you to know. I encourage you to read thoroughly. Since this is my first edition, I hope that you not only will enjoy it but also provide feedback.

You will be unlearning and learning some very cutting edge approaches to life and money management in this book. The concepts are simple and user-friendly. However, the strategies and methods go against conventional wisdom. For you to fully grasp these insights, you must ask yourself: Do I really want to be relevant and stay relevant in my retirement or be forgotten? There is, in fact, a direct correlation between wealth, health, and happiness for those with the desire to live life to the fullest. It's clear to me since you have purchased this book, spent your money, and are spending time; you are looking to live life completely. Searching for the answers is the first step. Second, is the openness to commit. You must be committed to staying relevant, to having a fulfilling retirement with purpose and opportunities for growth. I sincerely hope that you are committed to yourself.

As you read this book, you will need to consider another important factor in maximizing the opportunities to stay relevant in your daily walk. Information changes situations only if it is used, and to accomplish this, it must first get into your subconscious mind. When exposed to new information, there are five levels a person goes through when unlearning and learning new information. These levels are especially important for information that is the polar opposite of what is typically expressed in mainstream media and by industry gurus. The five levels occur at or through:

- **The subconscious mind**. The ground level where you don't know that you don't know.

- **Awareness**. You know you know, and you commit to this new knowledge.

- **Act**. The knowledge has gone into your subconscious mind.

- **Commitment**. The knowledge informs your way of life, becomes second nature, and small changes are made.

- **Arrival**. The level where being relevant becomes part of your life and legacy.

As you read this book, you will go through the first three levels. Upon completion of this book, you need to implement the information for a period of time before you reach level four and five. When you do, you will live a life, in my opinion, which is healthy and wealthy forever. It may seem a hard thing to envision right now, but this new path will lead to a fulfilling retirement – a relevant retirement.

Let's start the journey.

Chapter 1

ARMED AND DANGEROUS

Listen to advice, but follow your heart.
— Conway Twitty

Financial advisors seem to be everywhere these days. You see them in advertisements, as associates in banks or credit unions, and even on the Internet. How do you find the right consultant for you?

I've taken a scene from the 1977 movie based on the end of the 19th century in the Wild West in America. The plot focuses on the complex vicissitudes of the life of hard workers - a prospector Gabriel Conroy. Having found oil on his land, he knows happiness, disappointment, danger, and despair. I wanted to start the book with information that would arm you with the financial ammunition you need to avoid the disappointment, danger, and despair of hiring the wrong financial advisor. Finding the right advisor to help you navigate life and retirement should be simple, but it can also be complicated.

Most people simply won't have the time or inclination to obtain the skills for navigating the complexity of all their retirement planning options. Since you are going to hire an advisor, I have provided some insight on how *not* to hire a financial advisor. Despite what you often hear in the media or even from friends, family, or your place of employment, working toward a solid retirement plan is not easy. It's a good idea to get some help from a professional.

The foundational aspects of selecting the right person or firm to help you reach your personal and financial goals is understanding what to look for and what to ask. The first clue that an advisor is for you is whether or not he considers his clients to be co-manager of their finances. If an advisor wants you to hand over your life savings with the hope he or she has your best interests at heart, run — don't walk away. You are the only person who understands your needs and the lifestyle you want in retirement.

How do you separate the wheat from the chaff? One way to evaluate an advisor is to find out how they are paid.

Financial Advisor Compensation Models:

- **Fee-only.** The advisor gets compensated through fees. No commissions are paid, directly or indirectly.

- **Commission:** The advisor is only compensated when he or she sells you something.

- **Fee-based:** A hybrid approach of fee-only and commission. This type of fee structure can get tricky. With fee-based compensation, you can either be charged hourly, a flat retainer, or based on a percentage of investment assets. A fee-based advisor can also charge a commission on financial products sold to you, which could lead to a conflict of interest.

At the risk of loading you up with terms, the next few will define the types of advisors. You can read more about them at Investopedia.com.

- **Stockbrokers, broker-dealer representatives, insurance agents, and other investment advisers:** Individuals or a firm that charges a fee or commission for executing buy and sell orders submitted by an investor. They are regulated by the Financial Industry Regulatory Authority (FINRA) or by state insurance regulators.

- **Fiduciaries:** Investment advisors registered with the SEC or a state securities regulator. They take a more consultative approach in which the advisor is paid on a fee-only or fee-based basis. Fee-only advisors, in most cases, are fiduciaries, which mean they're legally obligated to act in your best interests. Fee-only advisors usually charge a percentage of assets (1%-2% is standard) or a project/hourly fee. Fee-only advisors sometimes charge both a percentage and a project/hourly fee. If disclosed properly this is fine.

- **Commission-only:** The "dinosaurs" of the industry. This professional only gets compensated if they SELL you something.

A new rule: The Department of Labor (DOL) Fiduciary took effect on June 9, 2017. It has both positive and negative consequences. The advisors like myself who are already fiduciaries will continue to advocate on client's behalf with the best possible conflict-free recommendations. Commission-based advisors or brokers will adjust their practices either to comply with the new rule or to game the system. Complying means going to a fee-only model and providing conflict-free advice. The other group will find ways to create new products that will provide profits for themselves and firms, making it business as usual.

The most common approach for this group will be to convince their clients somehow overnight, that they are acting in their best interest or have already been doing so, but they just happen to get paid a commission on some recommendations.

The worst of all solutions is for these advisors to convince clients who have already paid a commission in the form of a share, which is a front loaded investment, other commission type products to convert to fee-based and now pay additional fee's long term.

Even with this law, you must trust yourself and be your own fiduciary. This law is a great start, but there is a long way to go concerning financial education, unilateral fiduciary standards, and trust from investors as a whole.

Lastly, I believe this just confirms what I try to communicate in the escaping the middle class chapter – the poor will have limited access, the middle class will be over charged, and the well-off will negotiate an appropriate fee based on value. Trust yourself and don't just think because of the letters behind the name, or the fact that an advisor now holds themselves out to be fiduciaries you can blindly follow their recommendations. With all the information available today, your biggest job is to focus on only the things that are relevant to your unique situation.

Whichever type of advisor you chose, don't get caught up in the glossy brochures, fancy offices, media appearances, or suits. Advisors can also designate themselves with a variety of titles: financial planner, wealth manager, investment counselor, or portfolio manager.

A lot of letters may also show up after an advisor's name, such as CFA, CFP, PFS, CPWA, just to name a few. This alphabet soup doesn't in any way tell you whether this person is the right advisor to manage your money.

Treat the search for an advisor as an employer would when searching for a new employee. Here are some of the major questions you should ask a potential advisor, but you should add others that are pertinent to your particular situation.

1. What is the firm's investment philosophy? At this point, many advisors will launch into a long dissertation about market volatility, Sharpe ratio, or portfolio theory, which will have your head swimming. Don't worry about all those fancy terms. Even though they can be important, they should not impact the selection process.

2. Are you a believer in passive or active management? This is the best question to ask to find out an advisor's philosophy of financial management.

Active management requires an advisor to actively choose stocks, bonds, and other investment products. Think of active managers as an a la carte menu where your advisor has a wide selection of choices for dinner versus a passive manager, who is more like a fixed price menu with no substitutions. Active management costs more and includes lots of guesswork.

Passive is when an advisor puts most of your money into an index fund, such as the Dow or S&P 500. Fund indexes track prices of a group of allocated stocks. Passive management is "low-cost and no guess work."

Also, passive management has been giving the active management style a severe beating. CNN Money reported the S&P Dow Jones indices scorecard showed that 86% of active fund managers failed to beat the indices or passive funds.[1]

Also, Warren Buffet, legendary investor and chairman and chief executive officer of Berkshire Hathaway, is a believer in passive investing. He has been quoted in *Investor* as saying, "Don't try and beat the market with pricey, actively-managed funds. You're better off with a boring, low-cost index fund."[2]

3. What is your track record? How an advisor has performed in the past does not necessarily predict the outcome of future investments. The better question to ask is how long the manager has been in the business. Do they have women managers? Do the fund expenses and fees tend to be on the lower or higher end of the spectrum?

4. What is your background? Education is imperative in the selection process, but you should also inquire about credentials. You need to also look at the human element, such as core values and the ability to offer honest feedback. Your advisor should be focused not only on providing you with good investments ideas, but more importantly, guarding you against the bad ones.

Here are two questions you need to ask yourself:

1. Do I see my children or spouse working with this person? This critical question is often overlooked and results in having your loved one searching for a new advisor after a tragedy or life event. The issue is much deeper than the question: Can they work together? It's important to know if they will *enjoy* working together. Some client relationships can extend over generations. Having a good rapport allows for better opportunities for generational wealth accumulation.

2. Am I able to communicate and share my dreams with this person? Money can be a very personal subject – and even emotional at times. You need someone who can provide trusted advice. It's important that you and your advisor can commit, through patience, discipline, and collaboration, to making your dreams come true. Communication is vital. Without good communication, you and your advisor will miss opportunities to create the best financial plan for you.[3] You are now equipped to select the right advisor for your unique situation. It's official you are now armed and dangerous.

Chapter 2

Self-Talk to Self-Sabotage

"Positivity is like a muscle: keep exercising it, and it becomes a habit."
— Natalie Massenet

Self-talk: The act or practice of talking to oneself positively.
Self-sabotage: The act or practice of behaviors that negatively impact your life.

It all started with big hats. If you've watched any Victorian costume dramas on PBS, you know that women in the past had a penchant for outlandishly big hats. In fact, some hats were so big; women needed to duck their heads as they passed through doorways. In 1911, neurologists Henry Head (appropriately named) and Gordon Morgan Holmes decided to use the big hat fashion in an experiment. Why they thought this imperative is anyone's guess, but as it turns out, their research tapped into the mind-body connection. What they found was that even when women were not wearing their large hats, they continued to duck when entering doorways. It was as if the mind had stored the image of the big hat even if it wasn't there.[4]

It seems our brains are programmed to keep a mental picture

of our bodies so that we don't bump into furniture and can pick up a cup of coffee without spilling. Problems occur when the brain gets an inaccurate mental picture, such as in the case of anorexics, which see themselves as overweight when they are not.

Self-talk – and the way we do it – is also an important factor in our ability to succeed. The theory of self-talk has been around for a while. Recent studies have shown that it – with a twist – works. Psychologist Ethan Kross of the University of Michigan led a study evaluating the best way to self-talk. The report, "Self-Talk as a Regulatory Mechanism: How You Do It Matters," published in 2014, found that how you phrase your self-talk is essential. Saying, "I can do this," can cause more anxiety. Perhaps because this generates too much pressure and comes off sounding more like a lecture than encouragement. If you use your name instead of "I," suddenly you've gained distance and possibly sound more like a friend giving encouragement. "What we find," Kross says, "is that a subtle linguistic shift – shifting from I to your name – can have potent self-regulatory effects."[5]

It looks like Stuart Smiley of *Saturday Night Live* fame had it wrong with his self-talk: "I'm good enough. I'm smart enough and Gosh darn it; everybody likes me." On the other hand, gifted athlete LeBron James, who talks in the third person, even during inter-views, is on to something. James, for example, has been called out as an egoist for referring to himself in the third person, most mem-orably when James announced he was leaving the Cleveland Cav-aliers for the Miami Heat in 2010. "One thing that I didn't want to do was make an emotional decision," James replied when asked about Cavaliers fans' angry reaction to the move. "And, you know, I wanted to do what was best for LeBron James and what LeBron James was going to do to make him happy." Taken in context, his third-person talk may have also belied the star's efforts to control his emotions in a charged situation.

You may be asking at this point, "What is information about a picture of ourselves we hold in our heads and self-talk doing in a retirement book?" Although our perception of ourselves and the type of self-talk we use is important at any stage of life, retirement can be a time when you are looking to gain confidence. You may have a lot of ideas you want to make happen or passions you want to devote time to, but are anxious about making a move. You also may be hearing that annoying voice in your head saying, "But I'm too old to do that." When you start repeating negative thoughts, immediately get to a mirror and say, "*Your name*, I know you can do this!"

It's not just that the picture we have of ourselves can lead to negative self-talk. The larger problem is that negative self-talk and the false impression you carry, can create a dead end of opportunities. Getting to the point of self-sabotage can also hurt you financially.

Andy The Unhandy Man

Andy is an excellent example. As a young boy, Andy knew his dad could fix anything. He watched as he repaired broken lamps, dripping faucets, car engines, and anything else that could break around a house. Neighbors called his father Andrew the Handyman. No one can remember how his son, Andy, got the nickname, Andy the Unhandy Man, but it stuck. Whether Andy was too young when he first tried his hand as a fixer upper or was not taught the basics of repairing broken things, he grew up with the nickname and a feeling of being clumsy whenever trying to fix something.

The adult Andy now has his own house and family. Unlike his father, he pays someone to fix things around the house. The perception of his limited abilities impacts his finances. It's very expensive to call someone to fix minor issues within a house each time something breaks. The outcome of this negative self-talk is self-sabotage.

Let's assume a very conservative household expense of $2,500 annually for repairs over 30 years. Andy has a tax-deferred investment with a rate of return of 7% that compounds annually and new contributions are made at the end of each yearly period. If his investment's were taxable at a combined marginal tax rate of 29.5%, the ending balance would be reduced to $164,255. After taxes and 2.9% annually for inflation, the total would be further reduced by $69,672.The $2,500 a year for household repairs will cost Andy the Unhandy Man almost **one hundred thousand dollars** – money that could not be put toward his retirement. Do you think Andy could use an extra hundred thousand in retirement?

Not Good Enough Edith

Another example is Edith, a woman who has internalized negative self-image messages throughout her life. Being told she was "not good enough" has led to deeper issues. She strives to become a well-educated, well-traveled, and well-respected woman in her community, but something is always missing. She tells herself that she is not good enough or that she should be doing more for her kids, family, or company. These conversations then lead to retail therapy, image enhancements, or depression for which she needs psychological help.

We are also going to be conservative in Edith's case. Let's say she spends $3,500 per year on ways to improve her physical appearance and emotional health over the same 30 years. Assuming Edith has a tax-deferred investment with a rate of return of 7% that compounds annually, all new contributions are made at the end of each yearly period, and her investment earnings are taxable at a combined marginal tax rate of 29.5%. If her investment earnings were taxable at a combined marginal tax rate of 29.5%, your ending balance would be reduced to $229,957. After taxes and 2.9% annually for inflation, the total would be further reduced by $97,541. Edith would have "lost" a total of **$132,416**. Wow! How much are your unresolved issues from the past impacting your future?

Money Matters

No matter what economic niche you were born into, another common type of negative self-talk is "My parents weren't good with money, and that's why I'm not good with money." Based on this line of thinking this person could procrastinate or neglect to plan, which will result in self-sabotaging his savings, creating massive debt, and suffering from poor health due to stress. These outcomes will then confirm the self-talk of not being good with money. And the cycle continues.

If you think like this, you have tacitly given yourself permission to spend and not save because you have been told you just don't have skills to manage money because your parents couldn't handle their finances.

How about someone who grew up in a household where money brought out the worst in people? As a child, you may have witnessed people with wealth cheating or not caring about the consequences of how they gained their wealth. You may view money as evil, and therefore, want to stay away from gaining wealth.

Perhaps you weren't able to attend a major university or even graduate college, so you tell yourself that the top companies will not hire you. This negative self-talk could make you reluctant to go after the top job in your field, strive for promotions, or build strategic relationships. By having these self-limiting beliefs, you limit your income, therefore, impacting your retirement.

Unlearning Negatives

So how do we unlearn all the negative thoughts about ourselves to handle our money better? You must first ask yourself how those negative thoughts came to be. After that, you must use the work-sheets in the resource section at the end of the chapter to write down the negative thoughts and dissect them to discover the meaning and validity of those ideas. This is the start of unscrambling truth from fiction.

Phillippa Lally is a health psychology researcher at the University College of London. In a study published in the *European Journal of Social Psychology* in 2009, Lally and her research team decided to figure out just how long it takes to form a habit. On average, the research found, it takes more than two months before a new behavior becomes automatic—sixty-six days to be exact. And how long it takes a new habit to form can vary widely depending on the behavior, the person, and the circumstances.[6]

Sixty-six days is a long time. Rather than getting discouraged by that double-digit number, I suggest you find comfort in it. Make your changes in small steps. Try going 6 hours without any negative self-talk. Then go for 6 hours with all positive self-talk. Slowly you'll find talking to yourself positively will become more natural. Once you are on your way to positive self-talk remember this famous quote by Jim Rohn, entrepreneur, author, and motivational speaker, "Affirmation without action is the first step to delusion."[7] The key is to act on your new positive thoughts and become more aware of negative thoughts as they present themselves. Forming the habit could be the start of a better relationship with yourself and others. You might just reach for that promotion you talked yourself out of in the past.

What is self-sabotage?

Self-sabotage is the ignored elephant in the middle of the room. We all self-sabotage ourselves in some way, and for reasons known and unknown to ourselves. Cheating because you fear commitment to a potential partner or a goal you would like to achieve is one example of self-sabotage. Another is trying less than 100% on a proposal because you are afraid of success. Similarly, being unwilling to learn something new because you may fail sabotages yourself even further.

Here's the rub. If you are committed to staying relevant, you must commit to yourself first. Without having honest conversations with yourself and working through and understanding your fears, you will continue to follow old patterns and miss out on a retirement of relevance. Worksheets are in the resource section at the end of the chapter will help you work through this issue.

The path toward staying relevant just got a lot easier because you now know that you can start small and win big. With just 20 minutes per day of positive affirmations and self-talk, your view of retirement, life, and people in general, will change. I hope this chapter has given you fresh perspective so that you can implement the other concepts in this book. Remember to trust your gut. It always gives you the right answer. It's your mind that gets you in trouble.

Tools and Worksheets:
Self-Talk to Self-Sabotage

Download a full-sized copy of these resources at:

www.holisticplanners.com

LIFE LOGISTICS

THE FOUNDATION OF STAYING RELEVANT

Understanding that the only thing that matter in life are the decisions YOU make and people YOU allow to be apart of them.

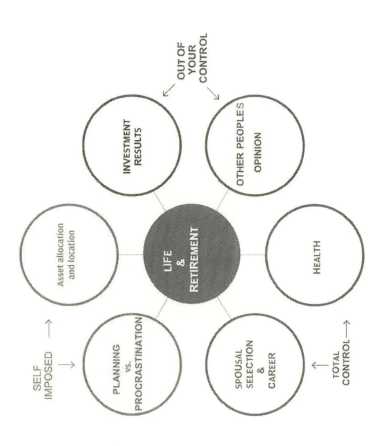

INDENTIFYING THOUGHTS

FEELING	SITUATION	THOUGHTS
Rate Intensity 0 – 100	Where were you? What was going on?	What went through your mind?

PERSONAL AND FINANCIAL GOALS

1. Reduce a fear
2. Having more pleasurable activities
3. Improving communications with my:
   Spouse/Children/Friends/Coworkers/Others (circle)
4. Expressing myself more assertively
5. Learning how to relax
6. Better managing my health
7. Better tolerating my mistakes
8. Better tolerating others' mistakes
9. Feeling less guilt
10. Feeling less depressed
11. Better accepting a loss/death
12. Increasing my conversational skills
13. Learning how I come across to others
14. Not taking disappointments so hard
15. Doubting myself less
16. Thinking more positively
17. Improving my sexual relationship
18. Controlling my eating or weight
19. Controlling my alcohol use.
20. Changing a habit
21. Controlling my drug use
22. Better managing my pain
23. Learning how to improve friendships
24. Reducing uncomfortable thoughts
25. Learning more effective parenting skills
26. Improving my sleep
27. Reducing my sensitivity to possible criticism

28. Talking about a pending decision.
29. Problem-solving/decision-making techniques
30. Reducing panic attacks
31. Increasing self esteem
32. Reducing family difficulties
33. Reducing job difficulties
34. Better managing my temper
35. Taking initiative more often
36. Receiving medication help
37. Decreasing procrastination
38. Better managing time
39. Decreasing trying to be perfect
40. Not reacting so emotionally
41. Allowing myself to express feelings more
42. Feeling more self confident
43. Discussing my thoughts of harming others
44. Adjusting better to a past recent change/incident
45. Adjusting better to a past incident.
46. Becoming more optimistic
47. Improving myself awareness
48. Adopting a more healthy attitude
49. Worrying less
51. Other (specify)

Now please review your list and decided which 3 goals you wish to change. My 3 most important goals are (write in the goal numbers):

First _____ Second _____

Third _____

What are conditional assumptions/rules?
(What rules/assumptions help you to cope with core belief?)

_____

_____

_____

_____

_____

What compensatory strategies are operative?
(What behaviors help you deal with core belief?)

_____

_____

_____

_____

_____

How do these beliefs and strategies result in negative or positive financial outcomes? Problems/negative affect/maladaptive behaviors?

_____

_____

_____

_____

_____

Top 3 Personal and Financial Goals Changes

_____

_____

_____

_____

_____

What are your motivations/expectations

_____

_____

_____

_____

_____

Predicted difficulties or challenges implementing concepts in this book?

_____

_____

_____

_____

_____

COGNITIVE CONCEPTUALIZATION

What problematic situations or roadblocks are you facing currently?

1. _____

_____

2. _____

_____

3. _____

_____

4. _____

_____

What are associated automatic thoughts?

1. _____

_____

2. _____

_____

3. _____

_____

4. _____

_____

What are core beliefs?

1. About self

_____

_____

_____

2. About others/the world

_____

_____

_____

Relevant childhood data

What experiences in childhood or later contributed to the development and maintenance of this core belief? Life or money

_____

_____

_____

_____

_____

_____

_____

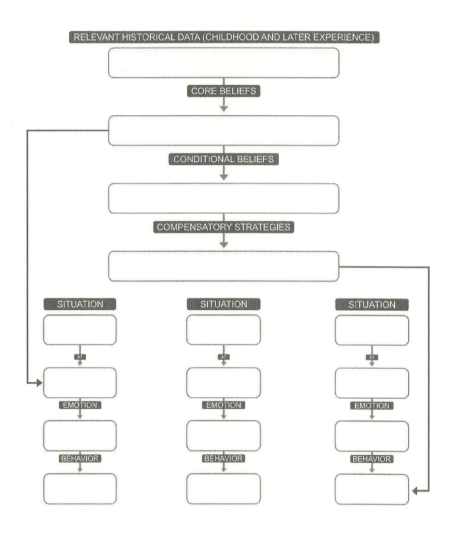

CASE CONCEPTUALIZATION

SOLUTIONS			
TARGET/ GOAL			
BEHAVIOR			
THOUGHTS			
EMOTIONS			
PRESENTING PROBLEM			

Common Themes in Problems:

_____

_____

_____

_____

_____

_____

_____

Underlying Beliefs:

_____

_____

_____

_____

_____

_____

_____

GENERAL PROBLEM SOLVING PROCEDURE

STEP 1

Define the problem and your goal in this situation in concrete terms.

The Problem is:

_____

_____

My goal in this situation is:

_____

_____

STEP 2

Generate as many solutions as possible. Brainstorm from your own past experience and from imagining how others might attempt to solve this problem. Consider a wide range of possible options.

POSSIBLE SOLUTIONS PROS CONS RANK:

_____

_____

_____

_____

_____

_____

_____

_____

_____

_____

_____

STEP 3

Evaluate the pros and cons of each proposed solution and rank them from most promising to least promising solutions.

_____

_____

_____

_____

_____

STEP 4

Try out the highest ranked solution. Make a concrete plan regarding how you will put this into action and follow through on the plan.

My action plan is:

_____

_____

_____

_____

_____

_____

_____

_____

_____

_____

_____

STEP 5

Reconsider the original problem in the light of what happened when this solution was attempted. If necessary, try out other solutions.

_____

_____

_____

_____

_____

_____

_____

_____

EARLY WARNING SIGNS OF LIFE OR FINANCIAL STRESS

Put a check opposite any of the following symptoms you have recently experienced.

- Sleep disturbance
- Appetite disturbance
- Concentration/Short – term memory problems
- Suicidal thoughts/Feelings of hopelessness
- Excessive self-criticism/Feelings of worthlessness
- Loss of motivation
- Social withdrawal
- Inability to make decisions
- Apathy and indifference
- Loss of energy
- Excessive guilt/Brooding about the past
- Agitation
- Significant mood charges
- Anxiety or panic attacks
- Decreased productivity
- Helplessness/feelings of having no control
- Excessive anger
- Apprehensiveness/fearfulness
- Negative thinking
- Loss of interest
- Difficulty feeling pleasure
- Other incapacitating symptoms not listed above.

Please specify:

_____

_____

_____

_____

_____

_____

_____

_____

MOST EXPENSIVE ADDICTIONS

"We can't control what happens but we can control our habits"

ADDICTION TYPE	ANNUAL SPENDING
Alcohol	$166 Billion
Smoking	$157 Billion
Drugs	$110 Billion
Overeating	$107 Billion
Gambling	$40 Billion
Addiction Rehab	$18 Billion

Source: Statistic Brain Research Institute (Online / Direct Response Mail)

"We are all rich most just don't know it"

WORLD POVERTY STATISTICS	DATA
Total Percentage of World Population That Lives on $2.50 a Day	50%
Total Number of People That Live on Less Than $2.50 a Day	3 Billion
Total Percentage of People That Live on Less Than $10 a Day	80%
Total percent of World Populations That Live Where Income Differentials are Widening	80%

Total Percentage of World Income the Richest 20% Account For	75%
Total Number of children that die each day due to Poverty	22,000
Total Number of People in Developing Countries with Inadequate Access to Water	1.1 billion
Total Number of School Days lost to Water Related Illness	443 million school days

CHILD WORLD POVERTY STATISTICS	
Number of Children in the World	2.2 billion
Number of Children That Live in Poverty	1 billion
Total Number of Children That Live Without Adequate Shelter	640 million (1 in 3)
Total Number of Children Without Access to Safe Water	400 million (1 in 5)
Total Number of Children with no access to Health Services	270 million (1 in 7)
Total Number of Children Who Die Annually From Lack of Access to Safe Drinking Water an Adequate Sanitation	1.4 million

Chapter 3

Look in the Mirror

"I'm starting with the man in the mirror,
I'm asking him to change his ways;
And no message could have been any clearer,
If you wanna make the world a better place,
Take a look at yourself, and then make a change!"
—*Michael Jackson*

Looking in the mirror requires courage and strength. Not looking in the mirror is the equivalent of a person who refuses to check the bank account for a balance, but continues writing checks, knowing all the while that they will not clear. It makes no sense to spend time pruning the branches of the tree of life or money matters without going deeper and examining the root. You must go to the source of your life and financial concerns to find out what would help you have the resources and choices to be relevant before, during, and after retirement. I'm asking you to do a forensic analysis of yourself to become acutely aware of how you deal with life and money. The actual work will begin when you review and complete the worksheets provided.

As we move through each stage of life, something is learned, unexpected social connections emerge, new skills are gained through jobs or passionate interests, and novel experiences are collected, hopefully giving us some wisdom about ourselves. Each stage can bring with it moments of reflection, a chance to look back at our story so far and reevaluate our life's trajectory.

The transition to retirement is a natural time to reflect. Inevitably, questions will surface: What was it all for? Am I expected to act a certain way now? Will I suddenly start carrying an ugly pocketbook around, like Sophia Petrillo in the *Golden Girls*? I still feel I have something to give, but what? How do I make this part of my life as relevant, or even more relevant, than my life before retirement?

The questions you have are exactly why, at this point in your life, you need to take the time to reflect on the past—all of it: the fun, the joy, the sadness, even that faux pas at Betsy's wedding – the one that still makes you wince. We all have a few of those memories.

It may be a little easier if we understand ahead of time that some of the intensity we feel while preparing for the next chapter of our lives is very likely related to what we went through when we were children. Even if our childhoods were relatively happy and stable, growing up always presents difficulties to overcome. A client once said to me, "I wonder how many retirees feel the way I do—trying to juggle getting ready for retirement while still sorting out my childhood drama?"

How we dealt with our earliest experiences has a lot to do with how we will cope when addressing challenges in retirement. For instance, if you had a difficult time with money or had trouble adjusting to a prior new stage in life, you will probably have similar difficulties while transitioning to retirement. A great Zen philosophy sums it up best: "What we do during a single day—and how we do it—becomes the foundation for our whole lifetime. For what is life, but the sum of our days?" Choices and decisions made during our life—both pleasant and difficult—never go away. They may become hidden, but they're always part of who we are.

To help with transitioning to retirement, reach inside yourself and try to remember what someone you loved said to inspire you or give you the confidence needed at a difficult time. Perhaps, there were times when someone in your life did not support your goals or actively put blocks in your path. Whatever you discover could be one of the most significant clues to how you approach retirement. How you overcame discouragement (or didn't) may influence your retirement. On the flip side, whatever has helped you before has an excellent chance of helping you through this next transition.

I remember when my client, Mrs. Frederick, said, "You know, Demetrius, in everyone's life there are times for reflection and re-capturing youthful memories, times for remembering relationships that seem so significant, and who gave us sage advice when we need-ed it most. Like the time someone told me that life could be like a car with a flat tire and the only way you can continue down the road of life is to get out and change the tire."

Taking Time

A client of mine found a way to give herself the best retirement gift of all. Each week she blocks out time for reflection. She doesn't make any elaborate plans, but somewhere along the way, she makes sure to spend an hour or more thinking and being grateful. We all need to create space to reflect, as this is the time in which our best thoughts are discovered.

Make time to reflect and think about the goals you want to

achieve while in retirement. Whether you think best sitting in a comfy chair, meditating, or going out for a brisk walk, shelter these moments as precious time for yourself.

Create a journal and jot down thoughts. If you're the type of person who wants to share your journey, create a blog and allow people to contribute their experiences or meet with friends to discuss the anxiety, excitement, and anticipation you feel. These are the emotions that can come with retirement.

You've looked in the mirror and decided to be radically honest with yourself, and you've scheduled time for reflection. The next step is to take action to control your personal and financial well-being. I don't know what your ideal retirement looks like, but I do know that you are the only one that can either create or destroy it through action or inaction. I believe after looking in the mirror, you will be happy with what you see. If you're not, it's time to make a change. Success comes from continuous improvement and self-analysis. Hopefully, the things you have read will help you stay relevant—in any way you choose to define it—for as long as you want to be.

Tools and Worksheets:
Look in the Mirror

Download a full-sized copy of these resources at:

www.holisticplanners.com

PLEASURABLE ACTIVITIES

	Do Now	Would Like To Do
Walking		
Exploring		
Being in the mountains		
Being by water		
Shopping (stores)		
Going to yard sales		
Going to auctions		
Fishing		
Hunting		
Boating		
Camping		
Listening to live music		
Listening to CD's		
Listening to books on tape		
Going to movies		
Watching videotapes		
Getting on the Internet		
Playing video/computer games		
Exercising		
Playing sports		
Watching sports (live)		

Watching sports (TV)		
Reading about sports		
Bicycling		
Day trips		
Vacations		
Collecting things (coins, etc.)		
Flower arranging		
Yard work (mowing, trimming)		
Talking on phone		
Painting (rooms, furniture)		
Drawing		
Doing crafts		
Painting pictures		
Ceramics		
Playing with pets		
Bowling		
Knitting/Crocheting		
Taking a bath		
Taking a class		
Eating out		
Golf		
Playing cards		
Doing puzzles or crosswords		
Other (please specify)		

	Do Now	Would Like To Do
Redecorating rooms		
Spring cleaning		
Reading fiction books		
Reading nonfiction books		
Reading magazines		
Reading newspapers		
Driving		
Watching TV		
Working on machines		
Woodwork/Carpentry		
Writing letters		
Writing (stories, poems, etc.)		
Volunteer work		
Gardening		
Caring for houseplants		
Singing		
Dancing		
Playing a musical instrument		
Acting		
Going to a party		
Lunch/Dinner with friends		
Visiting people (sick shut-in)		
Visiting friends		

Visiting family		
Doing things with children		
Church		
Church-related activities		
Praying		
Reading Bible		
Meditation/Yoga		
Playing board games		
Cooking		
Doing house work/laundry		
Cleaning things		
Cooking		
Canning & freezing		
Swimming		
Going to library		
Playing pool or billiards		
Photography		
Going on outings (park, etc.)		
Horseback riding		
Going to plays		
Sewing/Embroidery		
Other (please specify)		

Write down 3 things you have needed to do or wanted to do but haven't been able to do recently.

1. _____

_____

_____

2. _____

_____

_____

3. _____

_____

_____

Write down your specific target or goal for each of these

1. _____

_____

_____

2. _____

_____

_____

3. _____

_____

Target # 1

Steps: When:

1.

2.

3.

4.

Target # 2

Steps: When:

1.

2.

3.

4.

Target # 3

Steps: When:

1.

2.

3.

4.

Now write on your Daily Activity Schedule when you plan to do the first step for each target.

ACTIVITY SCHEDULING

At the bottom of the sheet under each day, write down some goals for that day. For each hour, write down what you did during that hour (activity related to the day's goals or other activities) and record your mood (0 – 100)

	Mon	Tues	Weds	Thurs	Fri	Sat	Sun
6 a.m.							
7 a.m.							
8 a.m.							
9 a.m.							
10 a.m.							
11 a.m.							
12 p.m.							
1 p.m.							
2 p.m.							
3 p.m.							
4 p.m.							
5 p.m.							
6 p.m.							
7 p.m.							
8 p.m.							
9 p.m.							
10 p.m.							
11 p.m.							
12 p.m.							

MOOD & ACTIVITY CHARTING

For each hour write down your mood (0-100) and
what you did during that hour.

	Mon	Tues	Weds	Thurs	Fri	Sat	Sun
6 a.m.							
7 a.m.							
8 a.m.							
9 a.m.							
10 a.m.							
11 a.m.							
12 p.m.							
1 p.m.							
2 p.m.							
3 p.m.							
4 p.m.							
5 p.m.							
6 p.m.							
7 p.m.							
8 p.m.							
9 p.m.							
10 p.m.							
11 p.m.							
12 p.m.							

ANALYZING THE EFFECTS OF CORE BELIEF

IDENTIFIED BELIEF:

_____

_____

_____

_____

DEGREE TO WHICH BELIEF IS CONSIDERED USE-
FUL (0-100%)

_____

ADVANTAGES OF HOLDING THE BELIEF	DISADVANTAGES OF HOLDING THIS BELIEF
How does it help me?	How does it hinder me?

REVISED BELIEF (ONE WHICH BETTER BALANCES THE ADVANTAGES & DISADVANTAGES)

_____

_____

_____

_____

_____

_____

_____

_____

ACTION PLAN

_____

_____

_____

_____

_____

_____

_____

_____

DECATASTROPHIZING

WHAT IS THE MOST LIKELY OUTCOME?	WHAT WOULD I DO IF IT DID HAPPEN? HOW WOULD I COPE?	HOW LIKELY IS THIS?	MY WORST FEAR

GENERATING ALTERNATIVES

IDENTIFIED THOUGHT:

_____

_____

_____

_____

_____

_____

DEGREE OF BELIEF (0 – 10%)

_____

LIST ALL OTHER POSSIBLE POINTS OR EXPLANA-TIONS. WHAT IS THE EVIDENCE FOR THIS?

LIST ALL OTHER POSSIBLE POINTS OR EXPLANATIONS	WHAT IS THE EVIDENCE FOR THIS?

| | |
| | |

Degree of belief in original thought now (0 – 100%)

_____

Is more information needed to decide which of the above is more likely or logical? Yes No

If so, how could this be obtained:

ACTION PLAN:

_____

_____

_____

_____

_____

_____

REVIEWING THE EVIDENCE

IDENTIFIED THOUGHT:

_____

_____

_____

_____

_____

DEGREE OF BELIEF (0 – 10%)

_____

EVIDENCE FOR:	EVIDENCE AGAINST

Degree of belief in original thought now (0 – 100%)

ACTION PLAN TO FURTHER TEST THE THOUGHT:

CHANGE/MODIFYING OR STOPPING

COSTS	BENEFITS
What would be hard? What would be the disadvantages or downside?	What do I stand to gain. What would be the advantages or upside?

Now go back over the items on each side and indicate with an *
or other symbol those which are especially important to you.

WORRY CONTROL

On this next sheet (1) list briefly the things which you are presently worried about on the left side column. Describe each worry in a few words. (2) In the middle column write down any action you can take to deal with the situation, if any exists. (3) In the right hand column, write down anything you can do to move on from obsessing over this situation (think of what might provide a good distraction) whether you could come up with anything in the middle column or not. Two examples are given below.

When periods of worry come on ask yourself if this is an existing worry on the list. If so, review what can be done and add any new ideas you may have, if any. If it is a new worry, ad it to the list and go through the steps as before. Try to move thinking about something else once you have done what you can do to solve or cope with the worry. If the worry hits at an inappropriate time (when driving, work-ing or with family) then schedule time later (worry time) to go through the stages, as outlined above. By doing all of the above, YOU ARE IN CONTROL OF THE WORRY rather than having it control you. Give yourself encouragement for taking any positive steps to-wards breaking the old patterns of worry.

SPECIFIC WORRY	WHAT I CAN DO	HOW TO MOVE ON
Not being able to pay the bills	Talk to bank about loan modification. Ask my parents	Work on my hobby (Woodwork)
Job security	Talk to boss, check new positions at work, search online	Get on the phone to my friend who makes me laugh

STAYING RELEVANT

SPECIFIC WORRY	WHAT CAN I DO	HOW TO MOVE ON

NO CHANGE/CONTINUING TO

COSTS	BENEFITS
What is good about it? How does it help?	What is bad? How does it hinder me?

Now go back over the items on each side and indicate with an * or other symbol those which are especially important to you.

LIFE OR FINANCIAL STRESS CYLE

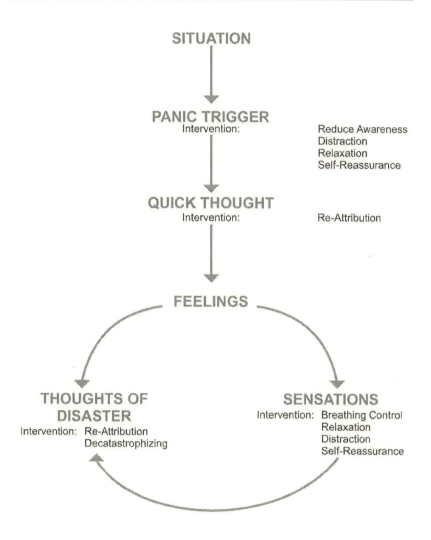

SITUATION

PANIC TRIGGER
Intervention: Reduce Awareness
                                 Distraction
                                 Relaxation
                                 Self-Reassurance

QUICK THOUGHT
Intervention: Re-Attribution

FEELINGS

THOUGHTS OF
DISASTER   SENSATIONS
Intervention: Re-Attribution   Intervention: Breathing Control
               Decatastrophizing   Relaxation
                                                 Distraction
                                                 Self-Reassurance

COMMITMENT TO MYSELF AND MY FUTURE

(This letter should be used as a template.)

I _____, take full responsibility for my role in creating the future that I desire. I understand the significant responsibility and will make it a priority. I'm committed to changing and measuring the items below to accomplish my goals.

I will:

*   Write a letter to my future self. (If above the age of 50, write the letter to yourself 10 years out and if under 50, write the letter to yourself 20 years out.)
*   Find an accountability partner within 66 days of purchasing this book.
*   Place myself before everything else knowing that the best version of me will be better equipped to be of service to others.
*   Work on my physical and mental well-being 3 – 4 x per week
*   _____
*   _____

I have read and fully agree to this Letter of Commitment and look forward to staying relevant.

Signed _____ Date _____

Print name _____

Chapter 4

Neurofinance

"There are two ways to increase your wealth. Increase your means or decrease your wants. The best is to do both at the same time."
— Benjamin Franklin[8]

Have you ever felt that the smart side of your brain goes on vacation when making saving and spending decisions? New research may suggest you are not too far wrong. It seems our brains are wired to sometimes overtake rational thought processes.

For years it's been assumed that the stock market is rational. When stocks go up the people investing or trading are rational in their choices, and when stocks go down, rationality also plays a part. Anyone who pays the slightest attention to the stock market, however, knows this isn't always the case. You probably have already realized market gyrations can occur seemingly for no reason. And guess what? Your personal financial decisions may be just as irrational.

The study of neurofinance, also known as neuroeconomics or neurobehaviorism, has begun to answer the question: Why does rationality sometimes go out the door whether you are a stockbroker, financial advisor, or a consumer choosing an investment or new car? Finding an answer begins by looking at the brain. With today's powerful imaging technology, scientists can now witness how our brains respond when faced with financial choices.[9]

Scientists have long been aware that certain parts of our brains "light up" or become active when there is an expectation of a reward; other parts of the brain shows activity in anticipation of negativity. In 2005 researchers Camelia Kuhnen and Brian Knutson observed brain activity using functional imaging (FMR). Their study found that activation of the *nucleus accumbens*, located in the midbrain at the top of the brainstem, the most primitive part of the brain, preceded "risky choices as well as risk-seeking mistakes." The study also found that the activation of a different part of the brain, the *anterior insula*, preceded "riskless choices as well as risk-aversion mistakes."[10] Marketers have been trying to activate your *nucleus accumbens* since advertising began, even though they didn't know that's what they were doing, to entice you to make purchases that are not necessarily good for your financial health.[11]

Overall, these findings suggest that two distinct neural circuits drive risk-seeking choices (such as gambling at a casino) and risk-averse choices (such as buying insurance), and that activating one of these two regions can lead to a shift in risk preferences. This explains why casinos surround their guests with reward cues (i.e., cheap food, free liquor, surprise gifts, potential jackpot prizes)— anticipation of rewards activates the NACC, which may lead to an increase in the likelihood of individuals switching from risk-averse to risk-seeking behavior.[12] A similar story in reverse may apply for the marketing strategies employed by insurance companies that court customer's risk aversion side of the brain.

The findings of this study don't give you a free pass to shrug your shoulders and say. "Oh well. My bad financial decisions can't be helped. Blame it on my *nucleus accumbens* and *anterior insula*."

Armed with the knowledge of how the wiring of your brain may be working (and not always in your best interests), you can make better financial decisions. Whether deciding between a McMansion or a smaller house that fits your family size and pocketbook, or coming up with a financial plan for retirement, you can remove the emotion from the equation and focus on the best financial decision for the lifestyle you want – even into retirement.

Chapter 5

Project Xero

> "Bankers know that history is inflationary and
> that money is the last thing a wise man will hoard."
> — Will Durant

Let's talk about debt. At any stage in life, debt will be the major obstacle to creating a healthy financial future. The two biggies that can sink your plans for the future are credit cards and mortgages.

Credit Cards

Many people have experienced a cycle of debt through credit cards. Credit cards are a must in today's world—purchases over the Internet require a credit card and, let's face it, sometimes credit cards are more convenient than cash to use for purchases. (Does anyone pay with cash anymore?)

Credit cards can also be a great way to track your spending habits. The monthly statements list all your purchases. Don't just throw that statement in the trash. Use it wisely. Review it each month to track where your money is going and what expenses are not necessary.

It's no secret credit cards come with a hefty interest rate for unpaid balances. Also, be aware that cash advances taken on a credit card often accrue interest at an accelerated rate. It's best to avoid cash advances, as well as to pay your credit card bill in full every month, to avoid mounting interest payments. Buying more stuff on top of what you have already purchased, but can't pay off, could get you into a vicious cycle of unpaid debts – debt that could take years to pay off. If you regularly can't pay your credit card bill in full each month, you're spending too much.

Mortgage

Owning a home can be one of your greatest assets. You get a mortgage interest deduction on your Federal taxes, and the house can be sold at a future date, usually for more money than you paid. Protecting and improving on that asset should be your goal.

The theory when I purchased my first home was *don't pay off your mortgage because of the interest deduction*. The rationale was that the deduction on your taxes would make a big difference in your tax liability, and would incentivize home ownership. So keep that tax deduction coming for the next 30 years. Boy, did that sound good. Even though the thinking has begun to change, homeowners still have the perception that the mortgage interest deduction is in their best financial interest. Let's do the math to find out:

If Loren buys a house for $200,000, at a 5% interest rate, she would be paying $9,933 interest per year. At a 35% tax bracket, her interest deduction would be $3,477, and her principal would have gone down approximately $3.

As you can see from this example, the interest deduction is

minuscule compared to the amount of interest you would save if you paid off your mortgage quickly. If Loren doubles up mortgage payments or occasionally adds extra dollars to the payment of principal, she can shorten her mortgage debt by years. Of course, when you are first starting out, adding anything extra to a mortgage payment will be hard, but as you grow in your career, find better job opportunities, and earn more money, it's a good idea to begin the process of chipping away at your mortgage. As you pay off more of your mortgage, each month you'll be paying more principal and less interest. It's exciting to see the principal debt shrink as you get closer to truly owning your home.

The goal is to be completely debt-free once you reach retirement (or ideally way before), so when your income takes a dive, without debt, a little paycheck will go a long way. It's best to begin the process of reaching zero debt as soon as you can.

Keys to Project Xero

The first step is the realization that anything that requires you to spend money without receiving income is debt. This includes:

- Housing until paid off

- Car, always a liability

- Clothing, if not paid with cash

- Children, until adults

- Vacations, if not paid with cash

- General personal and household needs, if not paid with cash.

Marginal Propensity to Consume (MPC)

In economics, the Marginal Propensity to Consume (MPC) is the concept that an increase in personal consumer spending (consumption) occurs with an increase in disposable income (income after taxes and transfers). The proportion of disposable income that individuals spend on consumption is known as the propensity to consume. MPC is the proportion of additional income that an individual consumes. For example, if a household earns one extra dollar of disposable income, and the marginal propensity to consume is 0.65, then of that dollar, the household will spend 65 cents and save 35 cents. Obviously, the household cannot spend more than the extra dollar (without borrowing). Simply put, MPC proves that you are likely to spend much of the money you get in a raise or bonus. It would be far better to use that money to pay off any debt, as well as to save more.

Project Xero Ten Commandments

When put into practice with an understanding of MPC, this very simple but powerful system can bring you to financial freedom in 12-36 months:

- Never purchase a primary residence that will require more than 28% of your monthly income. This debt-to-income ratio is called the "housing ratio" or "front-end ratio."

- Never purchase a car that costs more than one times your annual net income.

- Never save money in your 401(k) before you pay off credit cards or revolving debt.

- Save any extra income you earn.

- Invest in skills and knowledge.

- Purchase a home in a community with great schools. The higher housing cost will save you from having to pay for private school.

- Only invest in assets that provide income.

- Eliminate all non-income producing debt.

- Make monitoring cash flow a priority.

Friends and Family

Project Xero is also about removing all the individuals that are negative, non-productive, or non-supportive of your goals from your life. Ditto those that don't subscribe to your beliefs or values. Eliminating close friends or associates will be a very challenging exercise. To begin, you MUST make a list of the five people that you currently spend the most time with. The saying is, your net worth and income are directly correlated with the associations that you have formed. Some go as far as saying that you are the average of these five friends or associates. So, if you have four friends that earn $105,000, you probably make something very similar. The objective is not to find four friends that make a lot of money, even though that would be nice. You are looking for people who have the same core values, drive, and vision. Life is hard, but it's much easier with the right people around you.

Jesus had 12 disciples but he favored three - John, Peter, and James. Use this as your guide to make your selections of friends and associates.

Questions to ask when doing a friend analysis:

- Do these people have written goals?

- Do they have the same core values?

- Are their lives and family structures similar to mine?

- How much do they approximately earn? (It's not about the amount per se, but if you have four broke friends, you will most likely be the fifth.)

- Can I rely on these people for trusted advice?

- Do they have a history of disappointing me?

- Are we better because we know each other?

- Does this person cause me emotional or physical stress?

- Does this person motivate, inspire, or push me?

- Will my life change dramatically – positively or negatively – if this person isn't in my life?

- Is this person healthy – spiritually, emotionally, and physically?

Tools and Worksheets: Project Xero

Download a full-sized copy of these resources at:

www.holisticplanners.com

WHAT IS MY EMERGENCY PLAN TO DEAL WITH A FINANCIAL SETBACK?

(List everything you can think of in 4 categories: I can reach out to professional contacts.)

- Things I can do alone:

- People I can make contact with and what we can talk about/do

- People I can reach out to and what I can reveal to them/ask of them.

- Professional or professional responders I can contact

PREVENTION STEPS

What are some possible signs of slipping back which I need to watch out for (based on past experience or what I have learned in the book?)

List

_____

_____

_____

_____

_____

In the event of noticing any or some of these what do I need to do?

List

_____

_____

_____

_____

_____

_____

What are some high risk situations for me which could lead to poor financial decisions?

List

_____

_____

_____

_____

_____

What do I need to do to avoid or deal with these situations if they arise.

List

_____

_____

_____

_____

_____

Source: John Ludgate, Ph.D These worksheets have been modified for life and money management applications with the full permission of Dr. Ludgate.

All worksheets can be downloaded at www.holisticplanners.com

PROJECT XERO ROADMAP		
STEP	PLAN A	PLAN B
1	Pull Credit Report and Verify Accuracy	Pull Credit Report and Verify Accuracy
2	650 Credit Score and Above: Apply for 0% interest balance transfer and Debt Consolidation Loan through line of credit or credit union	650 or below: Apply for Debt Consolidation Loan with resources provided under PROJECT XERO debt management
3	Complete PROJECT XERO Asset and Liabilities Worksheet	Complete PROJECT XERO Asset and Liabilities Worksheet
4	Total Debt / 24 months	Total Debt / 48 months
5	Enroll in Micro Saving Strategy *See summary under PROJECT XERO	Enroll in Micro Saving Strategy *See summary under PROJECT XERO
6	Reward yourself after 3,6,9,12 months of success *Do it with cash	Reward yourself after 3,6,9,12 months of success *Do it with cash
7	Save the surplus	Save the surplus

Key Items:
1. Do not close accounts after they are paid off.
2. Do not pay anyone to fix your credit
3. Do not run up your credit cards after you get to zero
4. Do have a project zero partner – *very important
5. Do share your success with others after you get to zero.

PROJECT XERO ASSETS AND LIABILITIES		
Assets	Short Term Debt	Long Term Debt

100% of your attention should be given to eliminating these debts

Key Notes:

1. A primary home, unless it's a multifamily property, isn't an asset until it's paid off.
2. The faster you get to zero, the sooner you will be stress free and financially independent.
3. No one can fix your credit except YOU!
4. Assets – Cash, Savings, Investments, Rental Property
5. Short-Term Debt – Credit Cards, Lines of Credit, Car Loans
6. Long-Term Debt – Mortgage, Student Loans

SKILL INVENTORY		
UNIQUE TALENT	SKILLS / EDUCATION	MARKET VALUE

OBJECTIVE:

To assess your value through a lifetime of skill accumulation. Money is important, but skills are invaluable. Lose all your money, and that's okay, because if you have a skill, you can have it all back.

ESTIMATE YOUR EXPENSES

HOUSING		ENTERTAINMENT		GIFTS	
Utilities		Dining Out		Holidays	
Electricity/Gas		Sports Tickets		Weddings	
Water		Theater Tickets		Other	
Telephone		Hobbies		Total	
Cable/Satellite/DSL		Movies/Videos		Pets	
Maintenance		Clubs		Food	
Security System		Other		Vet	
Maid Service		Total		Total	
Lawn Service		Personal Care		Miscellaneous	
Garbage Pickup		Dry Cleaning		Other	
Rent		Health Club		Other	
Community Dues		Vitamins		Other	
Other		Prescription Med		Total	
Other		Other		Alimony	
Total		Total		Total	
Installment Debt		Clothing		Medical Expenses	
Mortgage(s) %		Self		Co Pay	
Student Loan(s) %		Children		Deductible	
Credit Card(s) %		Other		Medication	

Other		Other		Contact/Eye	
Other		Other		Dental	
Total		Total		Total	
Child Care		**Furnishings**		**Real Estate Taxes**	
Daycare		Indoor		Total	
Sports Activities		Outdoor		**Gifts Charities**	
Other		Other		Worship	
Total		Total		Other	
Food/Beverages		**Education**		**Business Expenses**	
Groceries		Private School		Other	
Wine/Beer/etc.		College		Other	
House Supplies		Classes		Other	
Other		Other		Total	
Total		Total		**Life Insurance**	
Transportation		**Vacations/Holidays**		Policy 1	
Loan/Lease		Airfare		Policy 2	
Gas		Hotels		Total	
Maintenance		Food		**Auto Insurance**	
Tags/Inspection		Entertainment		Policy 1	
Other (Trans)		Auto		Policy 2	
Total		Total		Total	

KIDS AND MONEY

The dynamic around the topic of money and how to approach it with young children often times is an opportunity missed. Many parents and grandparents tend to shy award from the subject because of lack of knowledge, bad experience in childhood or fear. This resource section on kids and money will provide tools to help you navigate the conversation.

Where to start?

First you should make it as non-threating as possible with the intention of it being a casual conversation. Before you begin understand where you got your philosophy about money from and make sure it's a positive one. If not make the necessary adjustment to correct those issue before speaking with your child or grandchild.

Thoughts like, money doesn't grow on trees, money is the root of all evil, money won't make you happy are a few examples of things passed on from generation to generation without anyone challenging those beliefs. This book has been about standing up to the status quo and this resources section is no different. Kids should be taught that we live in trillion dollar world and those who have skills can earn as much or as little as they want. You should also teach them that happiness comes from within but money allows you to share your happiness with more people.

Step 1. Allowance System

The value of an allowance system is to empower the child to be responsible for money choices. The allowance should be based on age, chores above the standard requirement for your household and family budget. It's not important the amount of the allowance but it's very important that you are consistent. This allows you to have a conversation around money weekly, bi-weekly or monthly. The power of an allowance system that is based on "doing more" provides a foundation for entrepreneurship and removes the employee approach. If you set up the allowance system based on minimums the child interpret they should get paid for things they should be doing with or without an allowance. This leads to entitlement and devaluing power of earning money by doing more than expected. Now that you've set up the allowance system how do turn it into teachable moments.

Step 2. Saving and Spending Allowance

Setting the common jar system or piggy bank works well for most households. This allows the child see in real time how money should be allocated. *Color coordinate the jars would be even better.

JAR SYSTEM	
Pay Yourself First Fund	10% to 20%
Charity	10% to 15%
Emergency Fund / Cash	25% to 30%
Fun Money	20% to 30%
Investment Fund	10% to 20%

Step 3. Use the world as your classroom*Make it fun

A few examples are listed below:

Teachable Money Moments	
Opportunity	Question
At the concession stand at the movies	Why do you think water is $4.50 at the movies but $1.00 at the grocery store? Do you think it's worth it? Example – Supply and Demand
Shopping Trip	Could you check the receipt and make sure we got the correct change.
Create a Budget	Discuss how earning and spending, wants v.s. needs work
Price is right game in store	How much do you think this cost? How do think it cost them to make it? Give examples and example margins Sale Price $4 and Cost to make it $1 how much profit will they make?

Step 4. Share with them how to avoid keeping up with the Kardashians.

- Talk about how things don't make you a better friend or person
- Talk about needs versus wants
- Talk about the power of delayed gratification
- Talk about being a producer versus a consumer

Step 5. Model good money habits and behaviors

- Talk openly about money and finance
- Follow a budget and share with them why it's important
- Show them how to avoid misusing credit cards can be harmful
- Take them to the bank when you make deposits or making mobile deposits
- Gain more skills and share with them how this impacts your earnings

EXECUTIVE SUMMARY

Most of us aren't taught about money at an early age. The key is to start as early as possible example the basic and power of money. The theme of your conversation should focus on making the subject fun, approachable and relevant. The biggest huddle is getting started. The resources provided should give you the confidence to start the conversation.

Resources

Board games
- Cash Flow for Kids
- Monopoly
- Payday
- Millionaire Maker – 10 and up

Banking and Investments
- Set up saving account without minimum and no maintenance fees
- Sharebuilders.com or discount brokerage account
- Google – Free stock market games

Research (Google)
- Summer Camps about Finances
- Programs about money for kids
- Work with your personal financial advisor
- Must view for parents and teens - How to Stay Out of Debt Warren Buffett Financial Future of American Youth 1999 (Youtube)

YOUR STARTING FIVE

11 Questions to ask When Doing a Friend Analysis

- Do they have written goals?
- Do they have the same core values?
- Are their lives and family structure similar or aligned with mine?
- How much do they earn (ballpark)? FYI – It's not about the money, but if you have four broke friends, you will most likely be the fifth.
- Can I rely on them for trusted advice?
- Do they have a history of disappointing me?
- Are we better because we know each other?
- Does this person cause me emotional or physical stress?
- Does this person motivate, inspire, or push me?
- Will my life change dramatically if this person wasn't in my life? This can be positive or negative.
- Is this person healthy spiritually, emotionally, and physically?

"People are either adding or multiplying to your life or dividing or subtracting. In order to stay relevant and realize your true poten-tial, you must eliminate those who are dividing or subtracting and quickly add only those who will add or multiply to your life."
— Deion Sanders.

SAMPLE LETTER

Dear _____,

We have been friends for some time now, and I truly value our relationship. I'm writing you this letter to address a serious issue, which is my future. I have some big goals that I plan to accomplish over the next 24 months and I'm doing a friend analysis per a book I read called "Staying Relevant." In this book it said that my future financial and personal well-being would be based on my closest 5 friends.

So let me get to the point.

I need us to ask each other a few questions to see if we will both benefit from this relationship. Whether we agree to remain friends or distance associates, there will be no hard feelings. Let's talk about our future and see if our friendship is in alignment with our long-term goals. Let me know if lunch or dinner is better.

Chapter 6

Investment Strategies by
Age and Stage

"The real key to making money in stocks is not to get scared out of them."
— Peter Lynch

Investing and saving strategies change at each phase of life. Each phase presents new opportunities and challenges.

Phase 1: Accumulation Phase: Ages 18-38

Postponing consumption by saving during an accumulation period will most often increase the amount of consumption one will be able to have later. The earlier the accumulation period is in your life, the more advantages you will have, such as compounding interest and protection from business cycles. In simple terms, this means that the earlier you can save money, the longer that money will have to earn interest, and the less impact any individual up or down cycle will have on the whole. It will also result in a larger amount of money at your disposal in the future.

This accumulation phase isn't just about saving money. This time of life is also ideal for the accumulation of personal and professional skills. The more skills you have, the more marketable you will be. Skills open up new opportunities, which can increase your income. Whether you stick with one company or are looking to experience other work situations, the more skills you gain throughout your life, the more you will benefit.

Phase 2: Stable Income and Accelerated Phase: Ages 39-59 ½

During these years your career and income have probably stabilized. You have reached your peak earnings. With higher income and stability, you should look to accelerate your investment strategy to make up for any lost years when you might have been more carefree about saving. These years are critical for preparing adequately for retirement. This is also the time when you may see sudden wealth through inheritance, divorce proceeds, sale of a business, or exercising stock options. (Read Chapter 15, Sudden Wealth)

Phase 3: Distribution and Income: Ages 60-70 ½

This is an entirely different animal from the first two phases. In this phase, you are going from the mindset of accumulating income to the mindset of having income for life. The investments you make in this stage must be able to do more than just make a profit. Investments should also be focused on protection. The goal for this phase is simply not to become greedy! An investment that gives you a 3-4% better return than another investment isn't worth the risk if you only need 5% to 6% to retain your required standard of living. Just like in the early phases, it's not how much you can earn, but how much you save. Put another way, it's not how much can earn, but how much can you afford to lose.

Phase 4: Generational Investments: 71-120

Generational investing is for those people who have implemented Project Xero and accelerated and accumulated assets to the point that the money from investments has shifted from income assets to next generation assets. This phase includes more advanced concepts such as trusts, alternative investments, charitable planning, leveraging assets through gifts and life insurance, etc. This is the best phase because you will be staying relevant to family and friends who you may never meet. Investing and assets go far beyond monetary value. When you can position, prepare, and provide for the next generation, you will forever be relevant.

Tools and Terms

To accomplish what you must at each phase, you must be familiar with the tools and terms that apply to investments in that stage. However, you'll likely find that most of the tools and terms apply to all phases.

Asset allocation: Just how will you divvy up your assets? Will you go domestic or foreign? Will you go with stocks, bonds, or something else? What will you select for your portfolio at each phase of life? Each of these is a consideration related to the *allocation* of your assets. The allocation of assets in the Traditional Model is illustrated in the pie chart below.

(Traditional Model)

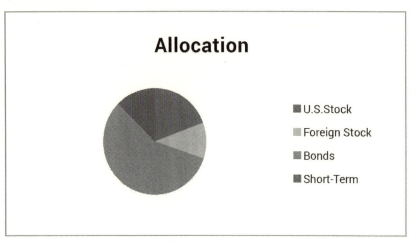

Source: Fidelity Investment[13]

	CONSERVATIVE	BALANCED	GROWTH
U.S. Stock	30	40	60
Foreign Stock	10	15	20
Bonds	50	35	10
Short Term	10	10	10

Source: Fidelity Investments[14]

Phases 1 & 2:

We allow our clients to go with either the traditional allocation or non-traditional allocation, which is a highly concentrated (index fund) until the third phase, the distribution/income phase. There is no right or wrong approach, but we've found that the index has consistently provided returns above 85% of active managers. Being highly concentrated within a long time frame will serve most clients well, especially those in the first two phases.

Entrepreneur Mark Cuban, in an interview with Alan Murray from The Wall Street Journal, said: "diversification, that's for idiots."[15] I would not go that far, but for those who are in the accumulation phase, over-diversification can be worse than having a concentrated portfolio.

The general thought is that the time allocated to picking the perfect stock could be better spent on investing in professional development courses, reading a book about your industry, or any skill-related activity which will increase marketability and salary. A balanced approach is needed, but diversification is only important after you have something to diversify, which is in phase three and four.

Phase 3: Distribution and Income

The diagram below illustrates the ways in which investment priorities impact each other as you prepare for retirement.

Four interconnected guidelines for the journey to retirement.

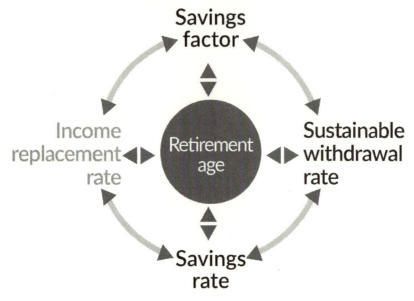

Source: *Fidelity Investments*[16]

The Third Phase is Critical

All these guidelines depend on individual factors and the age at which you retire. The average age for retirement had been 62[17] since this is the age when you can start claiming Social Security benefits. (Read Chapter 23, Social Networks and Social Security) (The average age has increased slightly for men to an average retirement age of 64. The average age for women is still 62.)[18] Waiting until age 70 to claim Social Security could substantially increase your monthly benefits and give you more time to save with fewer years to live off those savings. The age at which you choose to stop working has a significant impact on how much income you need from your savings. This, in turn, affects other rules of thumb like savings rate, savings factors, and sustainable withdrawal rates.

While you may not be able to pinpoint exactly how much income you will need in retirement, you probably have an idea about when you want to retire. If you're planning to retire early, you may want to use the rules of thumb for age 62 below. If you are planning to work longer, the rules for age 70 might be more appropriate for you.

RETIREMENT AGE	INCOME: SAVINGS	SAVE FACTOR	SAVE RATE	WITHDRAWAL RATE
62	55	14X	25%	3.9%
65	50	12X	19%	4.2%
67	45	19X	15%	4.5%
70	40	8X	11%	4.9%

Source: Fidelity Investments[19]

Guideline Assumptions

The guidelines for these models assumes a saver age 25-55 with $50,000-$300,000 in income or more with 50% on average invested in stock during working years.[20] To find your personal savings factor, go to the Fidelity Savings Factor calculator. (For an in-depth discussion about methodology and other key assumptions, take a look at the endnote provided.)[21]

Phase Four: Generational Investing

This phase allows you to invest as if you are in the accelerated phase because you are investing for future generations. The perfect scenario is that you are in excellent health and have resources to reallocate. Some advanced planning options are discussed below.

Self-directed Individual Retirement Account

This is an Individual Retirement Account (IRA), provided by some financial institutions in the United States, which allows alternative investments for retirement savings. Some examples of these alternative investments are real estate, private mortgages, private company stock, oil and gas limited partnerships, precious metals, horses, and intellectual property. The SEC has identified this IRA structure as having an increased risk of fraud.[22]

Internal Revenue Service (IRS) regulations require that a qualified trustee, or custodian, hold IRA assets on behalf of the IRA owner. The trustee/custodian provides custody of the assets, processes all transactions, maintains other records about them, files required IRS reports, issues client statements, helps clients understand the rules and regulations about certain prohibited transactions, and performs other administrative duties on behalf of the self-directed IRA owner.

The account owner for all IRAs chooses among the investment options allowed by the IRA custodian. For regular IRAs, these options usually include stocks, bonds, and mutual funds, but with a self-directed IRA, the term "self-directed" refers to the significantly broader range of alternative investments available to the account owner. IRA custodians are allowed to restrict the types of assets they will handle in addition to Internal Revenue Code (IRC) restrictions.

Generation-Skipping Trust

This asset is a type of legally binding trust agreement in which the contributed assets are passed down to the grantor's grandchildren, not the grantor's children. The generation to which the grantor's children belong skips the opportunity to receive the assets to avoid the estate taxes (taxes on an individual's right to transfer property upon his or her death) that would apply if the assets were transferred to the first generation.

Revocable Living Trusts

A revocable living trust, also known as a revocable trust, living trust or inter vivos trust, is simply a type of trust that can be changed at any time.

In other words, if you have second thoughts about a provision in the trust or change your mind about who should be a beneficiary or trustee of the trust, then you can modify the terms of the trust through what is called a trust amendment. Or, if you decide that you don't like anything about the trust at all, then you can either revoke the entire agreement or change the entire contents through a trust amendment and restatement.

Since revocable living trusts are so flexible, why aren't all trusts revocable? Because the downside to a revocable trust is that assets funded into the trust will still be considered your own personal assets for creditor and estate tax purposes. This means that a revocable trust offers no creditor protection if you are sued, all of the trust assets will be considered yours for Medicaid planning purposes, and all assets held in the name of the trust at the time of your death will be subject to both state estate taxes and federal estate taxes and state inheritance taxes.

So why should you use a revocable living trust as part of your estate plan? For three important reasons:

1. To plan for mental disability - Assets held in the name of a Revocable Living Trust at the time a person becomes mentally incapacitated can be managed by their disability trustee instead of by a court-supervised guardian or conservator.

2. To avoid probate - Assets held in the name of a Revocable Living Trust at the time of a person's death will pass directly to the beneficiaries named in the trust agreement and outside of the probate process.

3. To protect the privacy of your property and beneficiaries after you die - By avoiding probate with a revocable living trust, your trust agreement will remain a private document and avoid becoming a public record for all the world to see and read. This will keep the details about your assets and who you have decided to leave your estate to a private family matter. Contrast this with a last will and testament that has been admitted to probate - it becomes a public court record that anyone can see and read.

Irrevocable Trusts

An irrevocable trust is simply a type of trust that can't be changed after the agreement has been signed, or a revocable trust that by its design becomes irrevocable after the Trustmaker dies or after some other specific point in time. However, refer to Can an Irrevocable Trust Be Changed? for more information about certain situations in which an irrevocable trust may be changed.

With the typical revocable living trust, it will become irrevocable when the Trustmaker dies and can be designed to break into separate irrevocable trusts for the benefit of a surviving spouse, such as with the use of AB Trusts or ABC Trusts, or into multiple irrevocable lifetime trusts for the benefit of children or other beneficiaries.

Irrevocable trusts can take on many forms and be used to accomplish a variety of estate planning goals:

Estate Tax Reduction

Irrevocable trusts, such as irrevocable life insurance trusts, are commonly used to remove the value of property from a person's estate so that the property can't be taxed when the person dies. In other words, the person who transfers assets into an irrevocable trust is giving over those assets to the trustee and beneficiaries of the trust so that the person no longer owns the assets. Thus, if the person no longer owns the assets, then they can't be taxed when the person later dies

As mentioned above, AB trusts that are created for the benefit of a surviving spouse are irrevocable and, thus, can make full use of the deceased spouse's exemption from estate taxes through the funding of the B trust with property valued at or below the estate tax exemption. Then, if the value of the deceased spouse's estate exceeds the estate tax exemption, the A Trust will be funded for the benefit of the surviving spouse and payment of estate taxes will be deferred until after the surviving spouse dies.

Asset Protection

Another common use for an irrevocable trust is to provide asset protection for the Trustmaker and the Trustmaker's family. This works in the same way that an irrevocable trust can be used to reduce estate taxes - by placing assets into an irrevocable trust, the Trustmaker is giving up complete control over, and access to, the trust assets and, therefore, the trust assets cannot be reached by a creditor of the Trustmaker or an available resource for Medicaid planning. However, the Trustmaker's family can be the beneficiaries of the irrevocable trust, thereby still providing the family with financial support, but outside of the reach of creditors. There are also irrevocable trusts called self-settled trusts or domestic asset protection trusts that in some states, including Alaska, Delaware, Nevada, and Tennessee, offer creditor protection and allow the Trustmaker to be a trust beneficiary.

In addition, as mentioned above, the various irrevocable trusts that can be created for the benefit of the Trustmaker's surviving spouse or other beneficiaries after the Trustmaker of a Revocable Living Trust dies can be designed to offer asset protection for the trust beneficiaries.

Charitable Estate Planning

Another common use of an irrevocable trust is to accomplish charitable estate planning, such as through a charitable remainder trust or a charitable lead trust. If the Trustmaker makes the initial transfer of assets into a charitable trust while still alive, then the Trustmaker will receive a charitable income tax deduction in the year of the transfer is made. Or, if the initial transfer of assets into a charitable trust doesn't occur until after the Trustmaker's death, then the Trustmaker's estate will receive a charitable estate tax deduction.

Premium Financing

Premium financing is the lending of funds to a person or company to cover the cost of an insurance premium. Premium financed loans are often provided by a third-party finance entity known as a premium financing company; however, insurance companies and brokerages occasionally provide premium financing services through premium finance platforms. Premium financing is mainly devoted to financing life insurance, which differs from property and casualty insurance.

To finance a premium, the individual or company requesting insurance must sign a premium finance agreement with the premium finance company. The loan arrangement may last from one year to the life of the policy. The premium finance company then pays the insurance premium and bills the individual or company, usually in monthly installments, for the cost of the loan.

How do Cash Balance Plans differ from 401(k) plans?

Cash balance plans are defined benefit plans. In contrast, 401(k) plans are a type of defined contribution plan. There are four major differences between typical cash balance plans and 401(k) plans:

1. **Participation.** Participation in typical cash balance plans generally does not depend on workers contributing part of their compensation to the plan; however, participation in a 401(k) plan does depend, in whole or in part, on an employee choosing to contribute to the plan.

2. **Investment Risks.** The investments of cash balance plans are managed by the employer or an investment manager appointed by the employer. The employer bears the risks of the investments. Increases and decreases in the value of the plan's investments do not directly affect the benefit amounts promised to participants. By contrast, 401(k) plans often permit participants to direct their investments within certain categories. Under 401(k) plans, participants bear the risks and rewards of investment choices.

3. **Life Annuities.** Unlike 401(k) plans, cash balance plans are required to offer employees the ability to receive their benefits in the form of lifetime annuities.

4. **Federal Guarantee.** Since they are defined benefit plans, the benefits promised by cash balance plans are usually insured by a federal agency, the Pension Benefit Guaranty Corporation (PBGC). Defined contribution plans, including 401(k) plans, are not insured by the PBGC. If a defined benefit plan is terminated with insufficient funds to pay all promised benefits, the PBGC has authority to assume trusteeship of the plan and to begin to pay pension benefits up to the limits set by law.[23]

Alternative Investment

An alternative investment is an asset that is not one of the conventional investment types, such as stocks, bonds, and cash. Most alternative investment assets are held by institutional investors or accredited, high net worth individuals because of complexity and limited regulations of the investments. Alternative investments include private equity, hedge funds, managed futures, real estate, commodities, and derivatives contracts.

These strategies are typically for those who have maximized Phases One through Three. Most are investments that are long term in nature and include risk of principal. These can be very attractive investments but should be entered using only the capital that you can afford to live without, or, even in some cases, lose the total value.

	POOLED INCOME FUND	CHARITABLE REMAINDER TRUSTS	CHARITABLE GIFT ANNUITIES
Vehicle Definition	Charitable Trust established and maintained by a qualified nonprofit organization

Provides lifetime income stream to you or your chosen beneficiaries

After the death of the last income beneficiary, the remaining account value is distributed to the charitable beneficiaries you designate | Irrevocable Trust established and administered by your legal representative and designated trustee(s)

Provides lifetime income stream to you or your chosen beneficiaries

After the death of the last income beneficiary, the remaining account value is distributed to the charitable beneficiaries you designate | An annuity contract between a donor and a nonprofit organization

The charity guarantees lifetime income payments to designated beneficiaries

After the death of the last income beneficiary, the remaining contract value is distributed to the charity |
| **Minimum Contri-bution** | Typically $10K–$20K | Typically $200K or more | Typically $5K–$10K |
| **Income Benefi-ciaries** | Limited to 2 | Unlimited | Limited to 2 |

Assets Accepted	Generally at the charity's discretion; most types of securities and property can be donated, including real estate, art, and collectibles Cannot accept tax-exempt securities or mutual funds that hold tax-exempt securities	Most types of securities and property, including real estate, art, and collectibles, provided the donated asset can produce income	Ultimately at the charity's discretion; most types of securities and property can be donated, including real estate, art, and collectibles
Investment Management	Specific to program chosen; the sponsoring charity controls	Flexible; Trustee or delegate controls, depending on trust setup	Charity controls how the contributed assets are invested
Tax Treatment On Donated Assets	Partial income tax deduction based on beneficiary life expectancy and a Pooled Income Fund's historic rate of return	Partial income tax deduction based on IRS-designated rate tables (based on life expectancy) and payout structure	Partial income tax deduction based on a Charitable Gift Annuity yield set by charity and beneficiary life expectancy
On Capital Gains	Eliminated	Eliminated or deferred	Eliminated or deferred

On Income Payments Received	Taxed as ordinary income	Tiered tax treatment	Tiered tax treatment
Charitable Benefi-ciaries Number of Benefi-ciaries	Flexible if sponsor has a donor-advised fund (DAF) program — otherwise only one*	Unlimited	One
Option to Change?	Only if sponsor has a donor-advised fund program*	Yes, if in trust documents	No — must be sponsor charity
Setup and Admin-istration	Generally, no setup cost to donor; charity administers and may deduct administration fees from a Pooled Income Fund assets	Required legal setup; annual maintenance costs and tax filing fees; costs may be paid by trust	Generally, no setup cost to donor; charity administers; may not deduct fee from income to donor
Key Advantages	Easy to establish and maintain Eliminates all capital gains Potential income payout increase	Overall flexibility (if established correctly)	Easy to establish Guaranteed income payout

Key Dis-advantage	Fewer asset types accepted; income-yield risk	Complex and expensive	Inflation risk; locked-in charitable recipient; private contract with charitable recipient
Future Family Involve-ment	Yes, if a Pooled Income Fund is sponsored by a charity with donor-advised fund program	Yes, if a Charitable Remainder Trust names a charity with a donor-advised fund program as one of the remainder beneficiary charities	No

Disclosure: *For compliance purposes, I must state that each person's situation is different, and you should seek professional advice before implementing anything you have read in this book or chapter. This information should be used for informational and educational purposes only.*

Tools and Worksheets: Investment Strategies by Age and Stage

Download a full-sized copy of these resources at:

www.holisticplanners.com

JUNGLE MONEY MINDSET QUIZ

In this book you are going to find many non-traditional money concepts, and this is just another example of why money doesn't have to be stuffy and dry.

Find out how to navigate the money jungle by finding your animal type in the money jungle. Answer the following questions, and then follow the instructions to discover your animal type.

Choose the answer that best describes you in different life or money situations. Any answer you pick will be correct for you in that particular case and will help you learn how you relate to money.

1. The winning numbers are 29, 3, 4, 5, 6 and 8. You have the lucky ticket:
    ▲ Call my 25 closest friends, and we are off to Paris or New York for a shopping spree.
    ▼ I'm going to speak with my financial advisor and accountant.
    ■ I don't believe it and start to have an anxiety attack.
    ◆ I'm going to starting investing tomorrow.
    ● I'm going to give my church or non-profits most of the winnings and provide for family.

2. What I would say about how I handle my finances:
   ▲ It doesn't play a role in my life decisions.
   ▼ I'm an impulsive spender and like to treat myself as well as others.
   ■ The more I make, the more anxiety attacks I have.
   ◆ I want to be a millionaire so badly that I invest everything.
   ● I live by "You only get one life and the rest is already predestined anyway."

3. My thoughts about life and financial goals are:
   ▲ Saving for retirement is something I take very seriously.
   ▼ I need a better handle.
   ■ I don't have to be rich to be happy.
   ◆ If I have enough and family is taken care of, I'm good.
   ● I'm going to have the finer things in life no matter what it takes.

4. Project Xero / Budgeting
   ▲ use a spreadsheet or spending app to track my expenses.
   ▼ like the process of budgeting.
   ■ I don't need a budget.
   ◆ I hate being restricted by a budget.
   ● Paycheck to Paycheck.

5. How you would describe your cash flow habits:
   ▲ I have no plan for emergencies.
   ▼ The more I make, the more I spend.
   ■ I save as much as possible, otherwise I have anxiety.
   ◆ Money is everything.
   ● Paycheck to Paycheck.

6. How you would describe your financial plan:
   - ▲ Continuously monitor my income and expenses.
   - ▼ Don't even know where to start.
   - ■ I have an informal plan.
   - ◆ It's difficult to find the time to organize.
   - ● Financial planning is a waste of time.

7. My saving strategies
   - ▲ I should save, but it never seems like the right time.
   - ▼ Saving money is my passion.
   - ■ I have a lot of anxiety around saving.
   - ◆ I'll save what's left.
   - ● I pay myself first.

8. How do you feel about debt?
   - ▲ I tend to easily fall behind on payments.
   - ▼ I'm on project xero - no debt.
   - ■ Debt is good if you are using it for purchasing appreciating assets.
   - ◆ If I don't have it, I have no problem borrowing money.
   - ● I will borrow as a last option.

9. Helping my friends and family out of a financial jam:
   - ▲ I freely loan money without worrying about repayment.
   - ▼ People know not to even think about asking me for a loan.
   - ■ If someone asks, I would be open.
   - ◆ I'm not a bank.
   - ● If the interest is high enough.

10. Consumer debt (credit cards, line of credit)
    - ▲ I'm on project zero. No debt.
    - ▼ I have large sums of debt.
    - ■ I used a bridge loan to myself.
    - ◆ I have charge offs.
    - ● I only use American Express.

11. 3-6 months of emergency reserve
    - ▲ I'm living on the edge.
    - ▼ I'm living on the edge and try not to think about it.
    - ■ Tomorrow is always the day I'm going to start.
    - ◆ I have just about 3-6 months of reserve.
    - ● I have a year of emergency reserve.

12. Uncle Sam
    - ▲ I claim exempt or 9.
    - ▼ I look forward to a big refund.
    - ■ I hate paying taxes.
    - ◆ I file an extension.
    - ● I do tax planning to avoid being rushed in April.

13. My income would be great if:
    - ▲ No change necessary.
    - ▼ I got a promotion that paid double my salary.
    - ■ Cost of living would be great.
    - ◆ I believe I'm fairly compensated.
    - ● 25% increase would put me in a good place.

14. Investing in the market

 ▲ I'm a DIY investor.

 ▼ I don't believe in the market.

 ■ I'm conservative and prefer fixed investments.

 ◆ I work closely with my advisor.

 ● I'm an aggressive investor.

15. If I see something I want but can't afford it:

 ▲ I'll charge it and tell myself I'll pay it off with my next paycheck.

 ▼ One life - I'll pay it off over time.

 ■ I'll find a way.

 ◆ I'll purchase it but beat myself up about it.

 ● I'll walk away and come back in 72 hours.

16. Retail therapy make me feel:

 ▲ Great after a bad day.

 ▼ Puts me on cloud nine temporarily.

 ■ Causes anxiety and sadness the next day.

 ◆ It never happens so I feel great.

 ● Motivates me to make more money.

17. I'll take on debt for:

 ▲ Lower interest rate or to take a trip or treat myself

 ▼ Education

 ■ Business expansion

 ◆ Emergency repairs

 ● Only in major emergencies

18. I have anxiety around money:
    - ▲ Rarely
    - ▼ Frequently
    - ■ Always
    - ◆ First of the month
    - ● I'm flush with cash

19. Thinking about retirement:
    - ▲ I'm alarmed by how light I've saved.
    - ▼ I'm trying not to think about it.
    - ■ I feel very confident.
    - ◆ I have spoken to my advisor, and he states that I've done a great job.
    - ● I don't believe in retirement; I love what I do.

20. If I lost all my money, my reaction would be:
    - ▲ Panic
    - ▼ Denial
    - ■ Depressed
    - ◆ Motivated
    - ● Super excited about getting it all back and more

Notes

In the spaces overleaf, write the total number of times your answer matched the symbol shown. Example: 5 of your answers were ◆, 2 with ▲, 7 ▲, etc.

Each of the symbols represents one of the five animals. The most frequent symbol represents your money mindset. Use the answer key on the next page to total your symbols.

● ▲ ■ ▼ ◆

Number	Circle One Answer	Your Answer
1	▲ ▼ ■ ◆ ●	
2	▲ ▼ ■ ◆ ●	
3	▲ ▼ ■ ◆ ●	
4	▲ ▼ ■ ◆ ●	
5	▲ ▼ ■ ◆ ●	
6	▲ ▼ ■ ◆ ●	
7	▲ ▼ ■ ◆ ●	
8	▲ ▼ ■ ◆ ●	
9	▲ ▼ ■ ◆ ●	
10	▲ ▼ ■ ◆ ●	
11	▲ ▼ ■ ◆ ●	
12	▲ ▼ ■ ◆ ●	
13	▲ ▼ ■ ◆ ●	
14	▲ ▼ ■ ◆ ●	
15	▲ ▼ ■ ◆ ●	
16	▲ ▼ ■ ◆ ●	
17	▲ ▼ ■ ◆ ●	

18	▲ ▼ ■ ◆ ●	
19	▲ ▼ ■ ◆ ●	
20	▲ ▼ ■ ◆ ●	
Total		

TYPE	DESCRIPTION	EXAMPLES
	You spend more than you have and often live paycheck to paycheck. You always have the latest bag, car, or tech gear. Inside you long to be accepted through your image and things.	You have designer everything, your hair is always done, fancy car and you are broke.
	You grew up in a house where money was the root of all evil. What you learned is that you have to cheat or step over people to become rich.	You've been led to have a lot of anxiety around the subject and your prefer to ignore/put it off.

123

	You make excuses on why you spend the way you do or have an explanation for not being financially fit.	You want life to just happen and tend to pay the bill last minute.
	You have anxiety about money and losing money. You save everything so you are prepared for any scenario.	You were fully stocked for the next Katrina or Y2K. You have gone well beyond the required emergency reserve.
	You either grew up poor or well off. This provides motivation to never experience being poor again or to prove something. It's difficult to find a balance. So it's never enough.	Arthur Blank - Grew up Poor Oprah Winfrey - Grew up Poor *They are Billionaires George W. Bush - Grew up Rich Donald Trump - Grew up Rich *Presidents and Multimillionaires

RISK TOLERANCE QUESTIONNAIRE

Everybody has different goals in life. Everybody makes different plans to achieve them. The investment plan that works for your neighbor or your sister may not be best for you.

The first step to determining your ideal course of action is to determine what kind of investment style is most comfortable for you. Answer the following nine multiple-choice questions with the response that most accurately describes your attitude toward investing.

What type of investor are you?

1. I want to invest because...

    a. I want to preserve my existing capital.

    b. I have current retirement income and want to increase or preserve it.

    c. I have a significant financial goal to meet, like a home, my child's education, or a vacation.

    d. I want to accumulate a nest egg for my retirement or grow my long-term wealth.

2. My ideal investment goal is to...

    a. Preserve my initial investment regardless of market conditions.

    b. Generate income and achieve incremental growth.

    c. Gain moderate or substantial returns.

    d. Maximize my potential for financial growth.

3. I plan to reach my goal...

    a.   Within the next five years.
    b.   Within six to ten years.
    c.   Within 11 to 15 years.
    d.   At some point more than 15 years from now.

4. Over the next decade, I think that my income level will...

    a.   Drop, due to my retirement or raising my children.
    b.   Remain steady at its current level.
    c.   Grow faster than the rate of inflation. considerably.
    d.   Increase

5. Because of my level of comfort, I felt most at ease investing in...

    a.   Deposits.
    b.   Government or municipal bonds.
    c.   Blue-chip stocks, or those of established companies.
    d.   Stocks of new or innovative companies.

6. If the total value of my investments fell rapidly by 33 percent, I would...

    a.   Be extremely worried and concerned about the safety of my holdings.
    b.   Be concerned because I like situations with less volatility.
    c.   Remain confident that these dips should even out over time for long-term investors like me.
    d.   Buy up more stock because prices are low.

7. I predict that the investments I have today will double in value…

    a. In at least 12 years.

    b. Between nine and 12 years.

    c. Within six to eight years.

    d. In less than six years.

8. I can live off my current cash savings and investments for…

    a. Less than three months.

    b. Four to six months.

    c. Up to a year.

    d. More than a year.

9. I only want to own stocks of companies that are based in the United States.

    a. I strongly agree with this statement.

    b. I agree with this statement.

    c. I disagree with this statement.

    d. I strongly disagree with this statement.

Scoring: Give yourself 1 point each time you chose a; 2 points for b; 3 points for c; and 4 points for d.

What's my investor profile?

9 to 10 points:	Conservative
11 to 13 points:	Conservative/Moderate
14 to 22 points:	Moderate

23 to 31 points	Moderate/Aggressive
32 to 34 points:	Aggressive
35 to 36 points:	Very Aggressive

INVESTOR PROFILE

Conservative

These investors want to reduce short-term losses and seek a high level of portfolio stability. This type of portfolio could provide a steady current income as well as certain growth-oriented investments to keep up with inflation.

Sample portfolio allocation:* Bonds, 50%; Stocks, 20%; Money market funds, 20%; Domestic hybrid funds (stocks/bonds), 10%.

Typical investor: A retiree, or someone soon to be one.

Conservative/Moderate

The potential of returns and the extent of short-term loss fall in between Conservative and Moderate portfolios. This type of portfolio can provide stability of principal, steady current income, and growth-oriented investments to cushion against inflation and help increase the value of the portfolio for later years.

Sample portfolio allocation:* Bonds, 60%; Stocks, 30%; Domestic hybrid funds (stocks/bonds), 10%.

Typical investor: Someone nearing retirement and/or seeking stability of principal.

Moderate

Moderate investors want to invest for the long term and are willing to accept some ups and downs in their portfolio value over time. They tend to be less inclined to tolerate them in a shorter time frame. This portfolio is balanced between stocks and bonds to provide more potential for growth as well as possible steady current income and stability of principal.

Sample portfolio allocation*: Bonds, 40%; Stocks, 30%; Domestic hybrid funds (stocks/bonds), 20%; International/global stocks, 10%.

Typical investor: Parents who have both their children's college and their own retirement to plan for.

Moderate/Aggressive

The potential of returns and the extent of short-term loss fall in between Moderate and Aggressive portfolios. This type of portfolio may provide steady moderate growth over longer time frames.

Sample portfolio allocation:* Stocks, 40%; Aggressive stocks, 30%; Bonds, 20%; International/global stocks, 10%.

Typical investor: Couples starting families who have both college and retirement to plan for.

Aggressive

This investor is comfortable with a greater degree of portfolio risk and is willing to seek out the highest returns possible over a longer time frame. This portfolio tends to be almost entirely of stocks and can provide appealing long-term returns and the maximum level of capital appreciation.

Sample portfolio allocation:* Aggressive stocks, 55%; Stocks, 30%; International/global stocks, 10%; Sector/specialty stocks, 5%.

Typical investor: A younger, perhaps childless, person who will not retire for several decades and can therefore ride out many short-term market cycles.

Very Aggressive

This investor is willing to tolerate the highest degree of risk in hopes of greater-than-average returns. This portfolio is usually entirely of stocks, with some holdings in stocks of foreign countries or in specialized or cutting-edge companies or industries.

Sample portfolio allocation:* Aggressive stocks, 60%; Stocks, 20%; International/global stocks, 10%; Sector/specialty stocks, 10%.

Typical investor: A younger person just starting out, or an extremely experienced investor who is comfortable with a higher-than-normal degree of risk.

So what's my next step?

You should discuss these results with your financial professional. He or she will likely ask you further questions about your financial objectives, additional assets, and time frame in order to get as complete a picture of your situation as possible. Together, you can use this information to help devise a course of action that will best serve your comfort level and help you pursue your life's goals.

Traditional IRAs vs. Roth IRAs—2016/2017

	Traditional IRA	Roth IRA conversion	Roth IRA
Maximum contribution	• $5,500 (earned income) • $6,500 (age 50 and over)[1] • Reduced by Roth IRA contributions	No limit on conversions of Traditional IRAs, SEP IRAs, SIMPLE IRAs (if open 2+ years)	• $5,500 (earned income) • $6,500 (age 50 and over)[1] • Reduced by Traditional IRA contributions
Age limits to contribute	Under 70½ in the year of the contribution	None	None
Income phase-out ranges for contribution deductibility	**2016/2017** Single: $61,000–$71,000[2] Joint: $98,000–$118,000[2]	N/A	All contributions are non-deductible
Phase-out ranges for Roth contribution eligibility	N/A	N/A	**2016** Single: $116,000–$131,000 Joint: $183,000–$193,000 **2017** Single: $117,000–$132,000 Joint: $184,000–$194,000
Federal tax treatment	• Investment growth is tax deferred and contributions may be tax deductible. Deductible contributions and investment gains are taxed as ordinary income upon withdrawal. • If non-deductible contributions have been made, each withdrawal is taxed proportionately on a pro-rata basis, taking into consideration all contributions made to all Traditional IRAs owned.	• Taxes are due upon conversion of account balances not yet taxed. • Qualified withdrawals of contributions at any time are tax free and IRS penalty free: converted amounts may be withdrawn tax free.[3]	• Qualified withdrawals of earnings are tax free and IRS penalty free if taken after five years have passed since the account was initially funded and the account owner is age 59½ or older (other exceptions may be applicable). • Multiple Roth IRAs are considered one Roth IRA for withdrawal purposes and distributions MUST be withdrawn in a specific order deemed by the IRS that applies regardless of which Roth IRA is used to take that distribution.
Early withdrawals	Early withdrawals before age 59½ are generally subject to a 10% IRS penalty unless certain exceptions apply.		
Mandatory withdrawals	Distributions must begin by April 1 of the calendar year following the year the account owner turns age 70½.	None for account owner	None for account owner
Deadline to contribute	2015: April 18, 2016* 2016: April 18, 2017	N/A	2015: April 18, 2016* 2016: April 18, 2017

* Residents of Maine and Massachusetts have until April 19, 2016 to make contributions because of the Patriots' Day holiday in those states.

Source: IRS Publication 590

[1] Must be age 50 or older by December 31 of the contribution year.
[2] Assumes participation in an employer's retirement plan. No income limits apply when investors and spouses are not covered by a retirement plan at work.
[3] Distributions from a conversion amount must satisfy a five-year investment period to avoid the 10% penalty. This pertains only to the conversion amount that was treated as income for tax purposes. The presenter of this slide is not a tax or legal advisor. Clients should consult a personal tax or legal advisor prior to making any tax- or legal-related investment decisions.

Reference

Retirement plan contribution and deferral limits—2016/2017

Type of Retirement Account	Specifics	2016	2017
401(k), 403(b), 457(b)	401(k) elective deferral limit/catch-up contribution (age 50 and over)	$18,000/$24,000	$18,000/$24,000
	Annual defined contribution limit	$53,000	$53,000
	Annual compensation limit	$265,000	$265,000
	Highly compensated employees	$120,000	$120,000
	403(b)/457 elective deferrals/catch-up contribution (age 50 and over)	$18,000/$24,000	$18,000/$24,000
SIMPLE IRA	SIMPLE employee deferrals/catch-up deferral (age 50 and over)[1]	$12,500/$15,500	$12,500/$15,500
SEP IRA	Maximum contribution[2]	$53,000	$53,000
	SEP minimum compensation	$600	$600
	SEP annual compensation limit	$265,000	$265,000
Health Savings Accounts (HSAs)	Maximum contribution amount/over age 55	Single: $3,350/$4,350 Family: $6,650/$7,650	Single: $3,350/$4,350 Family: $6,750/$7,750
	Minimum deductible	Single: $1,300 Family: $2,600	Single: $1,300 Family: $2,600
	Maximum out-of-pocket expenses	Single: $6,450 Family: $12,900	Single: $6,550 Family: $13,100
Social Security	Wage base	$118,500	$118,500
	Maximum earnings test exempt amounts under FRA for entire calendar year/during year of FRA[3]	$1,310 p/month ($15,720 p/year)/ $3,490 p/month	$1,310 p/month ($15,720 p/year)/ $3,490 p/month
	Maximum Social Security benefit at FRA	$2,663 p/month	$2,639 p/month
Defined benefit—maximum annual benefit at retirement		$210,000	$210,000

Options to consider when retiring or changing jobs

There are typically four options to consider when leaving an employer's retirement plan, each with its benefits and considerations. Converting a portion of tax-deferred assets to a Roth IRA may be a fifth option to consider in certain circumstances described below.

Option	Potential Benefits	Considerations
Roll the retirement account into an IRA account (IRA rollover) (May also roll the Roth 401(k) portion of a retirement account into a Roth IRA)	• No income taxes or penalties for a direct rollover[1] • Assets maintain tax-deferred status • Ability to make additional contributions subject to income limitations[2] • Potential for a broader range of investment choices • Opportunity to consolidate multiple retirement accounts • If balance includes employer stock, may be eligible for preferable tax treatment (Net Unrealized Appreciation)[3]	• Loans are not allowed • Fees may vary, and may be higher than what is charged in an employer plan
Leave the money in former employer plan	• Not a taxable event • Assets maintain tax-deferred status • If you are between 55 and 59½ and are separated from service, you may be able to take withdrawals without penalties • Fees may be low depending on plan size	• Investment options vary according to the plan and may be more limited • Assets are subject to policies and contractual limitations of previous employer plan
Move the assets into a new employer plan	• No taxes or penalties apply upon transfer • Assets maintain tax-deferred status • New employer plan may allow loans • Ability to make additional contributions potentially with a company match • Fees may be low based on plan and size of employer (number of participants)	• May require a waiting period to move assets • Investment options vary according to the plan and may be more limited • Assets are subject to policies or contractual limitations of new employer plan
Withdraw balance of assets or "cash out" of plan	• Individual may use remaining funds (after taxes and potential penalties) for other purposes	• Upon withdrawal, account balance is subject to ordinary income tax on pre-tax contributions and investment earnings • 20% automatically withheld for taxes upon distribution • Additional 10% withdrawal penalty tax may apply for owners younger than age 59½. Additional federal, state or local income taxes may apply • Loss of tax-deferred growth of assets
Convert all or part of retirement account into Roth IRA (Roth IRA conversion)	• May provide income tax diversification in retirement • After taxes are paid at conversion, future distributions are tax free[4] • Required minimum distributions do not apply at 70½	• The pre-tax amount is included in gross income in the year of conversion (and is subject to the aggregation rule) • Sufficient taxable assets to pay income taxes owed is strongly recommended

[1] In a direct rollover, qualified retirement assets are transferred directly from the former employer plan to the institution holding the new IRA account, and no taxes or penalties will apply. If an owner chooses to receive the plan assets first, the distribution is subject to 20% mandatory withholding and the assets must be deposited into a new plan or IRA account within 60 days of receipt to avoid further potential taxes and penalties.

[2] Subject to IRA contribution limits: $5,500 / $6,500 in 2015 (if age 50 or older). Single filers may make Roth contributions if MAGI is $116,000 or below; married filing jointly if MAGI is $183,000 or below; phase-outs on contributions thereafter.

[3] With the Net Unrealized Appreciation (NUA) strategy, an employee may transfer the employer stock portion of a retirement account to a brokerage account. The employee pays ordinary income tax on the cost basis of the stock at the time of transfer, but will owe capital gains tax when he/she later sells the stock.

[4] Subject to 5-year Roth account holding period and age requirements.

A closer look at tax rates—2017

Federal income tax rates applicable to taxable income

Tax rate	Single filers	Married filing jointly	Capital gains & dividends	Medicare tax on earned income	Medicare tax on investment income	PEP and Pease limitations**
1	Up to $9,275	Up to $18,550	0%	2.90% (includes 1.45% employer portion and 1.45% employee portion)	0%	$259,400 single/$311,300 married AGI threshold
15	$9,275-$37,650	$18,550-$75,300				Pease: Itemized deductions reduced by lesser of a) 3% of AGI above threshold or b) 80% of itemized deductions
5	$37,650-$91,150	$75,300-$151,900	15%			PEP: Exemption reduced by 2% for every $2,500 above AGI threshold
	$91,150-$190,150	$151,900-$231,450				
33	$190,150-$413,350	$231,450-$413,350		3.80% (includes 2.90% tax referenced above plus additional 0.90% tax for earned income above MAGI* $200,000/$250,000 threshold)	3.80% (additional tax will be levied on lesser of a) net investment income or b) excess MAGI above $200,000/ $250,000 threshold)	PEP will end at $381,900 (singles)/$433,800 (married)
35	$413,350-$415,050	$413,350-$466,950				
39.6	$415,050 or more	$466,950 or more	20%			

*Modified Adjusted Gross Income (MAGI) is AGI plus amount excluded from income as foreign earned income.
** Itemized deduction limitation (Pease) and personal exemption phaseout (PEP). Does not apply to medical expenses and casualty or theft losses. Standard deduction is $6,300 single/$12,600 married couples. Personal exemption is $4,050.

Top tax rates for ordinary income capital gains and dividend income

Type of gain	Maximum rate
Top rate for ordinary income & non-qualified dividends	39.6%/43.4%*
Short-term capital gains (assets held 12 months or less)	39.6%/43.4%*
Long-term capital gains (assets held more than 12 months) & qualified dividends	20%/23.8%*

*Includes top tax rate plus 3.8% Medicare tax on net investment income beyond MAGI threshold.
**The exemption amount is reduced .25 for every $1 of AMTI (income) above the threshold amount for the taxpayer's filing status.

Alternative minimum tax AMT exemption

Filing Status	Exemption	Exemption phase-out range
Single/Head of Household	$53,900	$119,700-$335,300
Married filing jointly	$83,800	$159,700-$494,900

Federal estate Generation-Skipping Transfer GST tax & gift tax exemption

Top federal estate tax rate	40%
Federal estate, GST & gift tax exemption	$5.45 million per individual
Annual gift tax exclusion	$14,000 ($28,000 per couple)

Reference

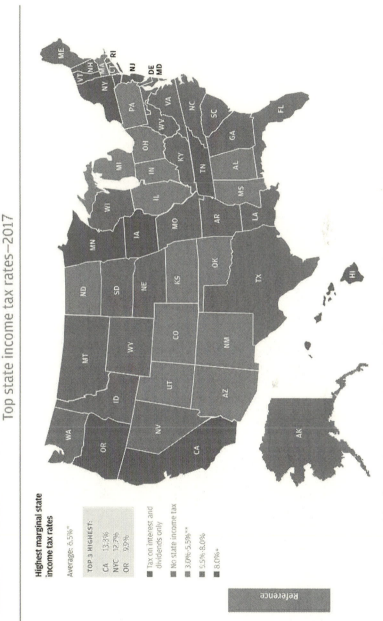

Top state income tax rates–2017

Highest marginal state income tax rates

Average: 6.5%[*]

TOP 3 HIGHEST:
CA   13.3%
NYC   12.7%
OR   9.9%

- Tax on interest and dividends only
- No state income tax
- 3.0%–5.5%[***]
- 5.5%–8.0%
- 8.0%+

Reference

Represents top marginal state income tax rates. CA top rate applies to income above $1 million. AL, IA and LA allow federal income tax deduction for state income tax purposes. Map does not include state estate tax rates or state tax on investments or trust distributions.

Chapter 7

Relationship Karma

"A successful marriage requires falling in love many times, always with the same person."
— Mignon McLaughlin

This chapter may very well be one of the most important chapters in this book. Why? Because being in a bad relationship will have a far greater impact on your personal and financial well-being than any bad investment. Take the time to read this chapter carefully before jumping over the broom or jumping out the window*divorce court.

There are 2.3 million couples who wed every year in the United States. That's roughly 6,200 per day.[24] Although the U.S. divorce rate has reached a 40-year low, a recent study reported that marriages still have only a "50% chance of lasting."[25] Studies have also shown that marrying the wrong person can dramatically affect your health and wealth.

There's a common reason why 50% of these relationships will end in divorce: spousal selection. One study stated that 95% of success is attached to the spousal selection. While couples intend to stay married when they tie the knot, many couples find it challenging to obtain the happily ever after.

Marketing Marriage

Businesses and marketers have devoted billions of dollars to activate your *nucleus accumbens,* your brain's reward center, (Read Chapter 4, Neurofinance) to convince couples to spend thousands of dollars on the one-day experience of a wedding. In 2016 the average wedding cost was over $35,000 and took more than a year to plan.[26] Imagine if that $35,000 was used for a down payment on a house. If invested, think how much you would have 20, 30 years down the road.

If you divorce you lose more money. Splitsville comes with a significant impact on financial and personal well-being. Studies have shown marrying the wrong person can dramatically affect your health and wealth.[27] In this chapter, you will find a tool to help you navigate the most important decision in your life: Who you will spend your life with. Chose the wrong person and you may be looking at a life of stress, which can bring on chronic disease, fatigue, and depression. If you decide to divorce, your finances and retirement could be compromised.

Divorce

With Internet dating and social media it's getting easier to find a partner. Staying married and being happy is a different ballgame. Northwestern University psychology professor Eli Finkel states that marriage is currently both the most and the least satisfying institution that has ever been. "Americans today have elevated their expectations for marriage and can, in fact, achieve an unprecedentedly high level of marital quality," he writes, "but only if they invest a lot of effort. And if they can't, their marriage will be more disappointing to them than a humdrum marriage was to prior generations, because they've been promised so much more."[28]

Wifey and Hubby Score

I have developed what I call, "Your Wifey or Hubby Score," to provide couples with a standardized, reliable, and common sense approach that is often not utilized to measure an individual's financial and relational well-being. I've tested this set of questions to measure financial and relationship well-being. The questions are designed to uncover an individual's life philosophy, likes and dislikes, goals, and core values. The score is based on a range that is calculated from the answers, which will clarify whether or not your intended is marriageable material for you – something that is not directly evident when looking through rose-colored glasses. I also hope that taking this quiz as a couple will create an opportunity for in-depth conversations and discussions. A Wifey and Hubby questionnaire is included in this book as well as on the website www.h olisticplanners.com.

The Wifey and Hubby Score

- A non-emotional, purely intellectual score based on proprietary methods that draws on insights from happy couples married longer than 30 years, as well as experts in the field.

- A key indicating tool developed using nontraditional methods, including cognitive behavioral trends and testing, to ensure accurate comprehension of questions.

- The quiz is for entertainment purposes only and should not be considered professional advice. I believe it is highly reliable and a valid measurement of readiness and compatibility for marriage.

- The scoring method used for calculating each score is inclusive of many factors, subjective and non-subjective. The approach is a statistical and human dynamic method that provides a more accurate measure than a simple summary score. It offers both a score and a detailed report. This approach gives more accurate individual estimates because it allows different items in a range, and people's responses to these questions, to contribute differently to the final score.

- A scoring system that is flexible and based on different dynamics should allow for variation in individual preferences and goals. This methodology is complex, but an easy way to measure important, yet traditionally hard to quantify success factors like feelings of engagement, security, and satisfaction. This methodology can be utilized as a benchmark across very different types of relationships.

The Scoring Process

Once an individual or a couple completes the questionnaire, determining your Wifey or Hubby Score is done in 2 steps:

Determining the Wifey or Hubby Score

Step 1: Using the scoring worksheet, enter a number from 0 to 75 that corresponds to each of your responses into the right-hand column. Add them up to find the Wifey or Hubby Score you will use in Step 2.

Step 2: Convert the total score. On the second page of the scoring worksheet, locate the total response value from Step 1 in the first column, then follow the row across to the appropriate column based on your age group and whether or not you read the questionnaire to yourself (self-administered), or had the questions read to you by your mate, friend, or partner (administered by someone else). This will give you your Wifey or Hubby Score. (The scoring worksheet is available in Appendix A at the end of this book. For more detailed instructions about the two-step scoring process, including step-by-step examples showing how to score different age groups and survey modes, see Section 1: Scoring Key. It is important to note that the quiz can only be scored using the scoring worksheet if you provided an answer to all questions on the quiz. Any responses such as "rather not answer" or skipped questions make the use of the look-up table inaccurate.)

Interpreting the score

A Wifey or Hubby Score is a standardized number like a credit score from a low of 250 to a high of 900. It represents your underlying level of Wifey or Hubby potential. The number doesn't define you or have any meaning on its own. Most scores will fall somewhere in the middle.

Frequently asked questions

- **Why is the scoring different for different age groups?** I wanted to create a system for all phases of life that could be used by both working age and older adults, including those in retirement. Based on research and testing, I determined that individuals did answer the questions slightly differently depending on their age group (i.e. Millennials, X and Y, and Boomers 62+).

- **Why is the scoring different for different modes?** Based on my research and testing, I have determined that the quiz-takers did answer questions on the Wifey and Hubby Score differently depending on whether they were administered the questions via phone or they self-administered the quiz using a computer. Step 2 of the scoring worksheet takes these mode-related differences into account and converts the raw total to a "normalized" score that is then directly comparable across the modes.

- **Can I force my future wife or husband to do this if he or she doesn't want too?** No. (BIG RED FLAG.) For the scoring methods outlined in this book, it is necessary for you and your mate to provide an answer to every item on the questionnaire. It is not possible to accurately score individuals who do not respond to all the issues with the two-step process, as skipping items reduces the overall number of items measured. (For instance, an individual who answered all of the questions and has a total response value of 30 out of 40 likely does not have the same spousal potential as an individual who skipped two of the items and therefore has a total response value of 30 out of 32.)

- **What is a good (or bad) score?** Scores are neither good nor bad. All scores are benchmarks that serve as guides to improving yourself, as well as your relationship. However, as you understand and share your Wifey or Hubby Score with future mates, you may be able to establish benchmarks, as well as to analyze your patterns in relation to other life experiences you may have with other relationships. It is also important to note that small changes in scores due to answering a few questions slightly differently may result in movements up or down the spectrum that do not necessarily indicate a meaningful change in underlying spousal potential. Each estimated value on the Wifey or Hubby Score is measured with some error, so small variations in a person's score should be interpreted carefully.

This methodology is based on the results of seeing how the wrong or right spousal selection can impact retirement or financial plans. I hope you find the questionnaire helpful.

Tools and Worksheets: Relationship Karma

Download a full-sized copy of these resources at:

www.holisticplanners.com

WIFEY AND HUBBY QUIZ

Instructions: Please answer all questions truthfully and thoughtfully.

1. Date of Birth (mm/dd/yy) _____

2. Race _____

3. Sex? Male or Female _____

4. How frequently do you have an alcoholic beverage?
   A. Never
   B. Socially 1-3 per week
   C. Frequently with dinner or after work
   D. Happy Hour – Special Events

5. How many sex partners have you had?
   A. Virgin
   B. 1-3
   C. 3-9
   D. 9+

6. Do you have a passport?
   A. Yes
   B. No

7. Have you ever been emotionally, physically, or sexually abused as a child or adult?
   A. Yes
   B. No

8. How many children do have?
   A. None
   B. 1
   C. 2
   D. 3 or more

9. How many children do you want?
   A. None
   B. 1
   C. 2
   D. 3 or more

10. Height and Weight?

_____

11. Have you ever had a prolonged phase of sadness or depression?

_____

12. Have you or any family member been treated (past or current) for any mental health challenges?

_____

13. Highest level of education?
   A. High School
   B. Bachelors
   C. Masters
   D. Ph.D.

14. Current Income?
    A. Below 50,000
    B. 50,000-100,000
    C. 100,001-250,000
    D. 250,000 or more

15. Number hours spent on social media or watching television weekly?
    A. None
    B. 1-5 hours per week
    C. 5-10 hours per week
    D. 10 or more

16. How often do you prepare your own meals?
    A. Never
    B. 1-2 times per week
    C. 3-5 times per week
    D. Every day

17. Were both parents in the household?
    A. Yes, still married
    B. Yes, divorced
    C. No, never married
    D. No, other

18. Current credit score?
    A. 350-500
    B. 501-650
    C. 651-725
    D. 726-850

19. Do you like pets?
   A. Slightly
   B. Love animals
   C. Indifferent
   D. Hate them or Allergic

20. Have you or would you discuss a non-monogamous relationship?
   A. No
   B. Yes
   C. Never
   D. Maybe

21. Religion?
   A. Christian
   B. Muslim
   C. Jewish
   D. Catholic
   E. Other

22. How often do you work out?
   A. Never
   B. Occasionally
   C. Often
   D. Gym Rat

23. How would you rate your current happiness?
   A. Totally Happy
   B. Somewhat Happy
   C. Fair
   D. Unhappy

24. How often do you attend social events?

    A. Frequently

    B. When necessary

    C. Not Often

    D. Work Related Only

25. What's your level of confidence in financial matters?

    A. Poor

    B. Fair

    C. Good

    D. Great

26. Describe your money habits?

    A. Frugal

    B. Budget minded

    C. Live for Today

    D. Spend until it's gone

27. How often do you say hurtful things when angry?

    A. Never

    B. Sometimes

    C. Most of time

    D. Always

28. When angry, how often do you blow up and don't know how to express your feelings?

    A. Never

    B. Sometimes

    C. Most of time

    D. Always

29. How serious are you about you career?

    A. Totally Focused

    B. Somewhat Focused

    C. Take it as it comes

    D. More focused on life and balance

30. Which statement describes you (or how you would describe your spouse in 5 years)?

    A. Housewife

    B. Modern Day Working Woman

    C. Feminist

    D. Trophy Wife

31. Which statement describes you (or how would describe your spouse in 5 years)?

    A. Father and Provider

    B. On the Executive Track

    C. Stay at Home Dad

    D. Adventurer and Husband

32. What percent of your friends are married?

    A. None

    B. Few

    C. Many

    D. All

33. What percent of your friends have a college or advanced degrees?

    A. None

    B. Few

    C. Many

D. All

34. How do you feel about paying / being financial responsible for everything?
A. Totally Comfortable
B. Uncomfortable
C. Doable
D. Resentful

35. I believe in traditional gender roles?
A. Agree
B. Disagree
C. On the fence
D. Depends

36. A man should be the protector and provider?
A. Agree
B. Disagree
C. On the fence
D. Depends

37. A woman should be the caretaker and provide emotional support?
A. Agree
B. Disagree
C. On the fence
D. Depends

38. Which diet is most aligned with your daily habits?
A. Vegetarian
B. Vegan

C. Anything goes

D. Healthy eating mostly

39. Which describes you best?

A. Homebody

B. Adventurer

C. Workaholic

D. Big Kid

40. Have many books do you read a year?

A. None

B. 1-2

C. 3-4

D. 5 or more

41. How would you support you partners career or life goals?

A. Encourage them to go for it

B. Actively engage in seeing how you can give support

C. Secretly resent them

D. Support from afar while pursuing your own goals

42. Which best describes you?

A. I can be bored easily

B. I'm very loyal

C. I'm a person who seeks to please others

D. I'm a person who needs to be center of the action

43. If your marriage experiences a difficult period, how would you handle it?

A. Seek professional help

B. Ask a parent for advice

C. Ask a friend for advice

D. Work it out with your spouse or go it alone

44. How similar are your partner's career?

A. Similar

B. Somewhat Similar

C. Totally Different

D. Totally the Same

45. How similar are your interests, i.e. hobbies, art, literature?

A. Similar

B. Somewhat Similar

C. Totally Different

D. Totally the Same

46. What do you consider enough time to find your passion or find your career path?

A. 0-5 years

B. 6-10 years

C. 11-15 years

D. Unlimited

47. Is cheating a forgivable experience?

A. Maybe

B. Yes

C. Yes, with time and professional help

D. Never

48. Do you get along with in-laws?
- A. Little friction
- B. Somewhat
- C. Hate them
- D. Love them

49. Have any of your siblings been divorced?
- A. No
- B. Yes
- C. Yes, but remarried
- D. Yes, multiple times

50. Could you see yourself 50lbs and 50 years later with this person?
- A. No
- B. Maybe
- C. Yes, with conditions
- D. Yes, without conditions

Request your full score and report at relationshipkarma.com

NEW COUPLE GUIDE

TOP 10 STEPS

- Pull credit report and exchange with future spouse. (Discuss in detail)
- Create debt repayment plan (See project xero)
- Create individual and joint budgets (included)
- Create cash flow system – Track all spending
- Create saving plan – Save an specific amount monthly before paying any bills
- Create goal sheet i.e. save x for down payment, save y for new car etc
- Review all accounts online weekly
- Take – The Wifey and Hubby Quiz
- Discuss Family Health History * #1 financial reason for financial hardship
- Create mission statement and ideal marital focus (short and long term goals) i.e. kids, locations, religion etc

Chapter 8

Life Goes On

"Life is pleasant. Death is peaceful. It's the transition that's troublesome."
— Isaac Asimov

Death of a Spouse

Your world changes when your spouse dies. You are in mourning—feeling grief and sorrow at the loss. You may feel numb, shocked, and fearful. You may feel guilty for being the one who is still alive. At some point, you may even feel angry at your spouse for leaving you. All of these feelings are normal. There are no rules about how you should feel. There is no right or wrong way to mourn.

You can feel both physical and emotional pain when you grieve. People who are grieving often cry easily and can have:

- Trouble sleeping
- Little interest in food
- Problems with concentration
- A hard time making decisions

159

In addition to dealing with feelings of loss, you may also need to put your own life back together. This can be hard work. Some people feel better sooner than they expect. Others may take longer. Family, friends, and faith may be sources of support. Grief counseling or grief therapy is also helpful for some people.

As time passes, you may still miss your spouse, but the intense pain will lessen. There will be good and bad days. You will know you are feeling better when there are more good days than bad. Don't feel guilty if you laugh at a joke or enjoy a visit with a friend.

For some people, mourning can go on so long that it becomes unhealthy. This can be a sign of serious depression or anxiety. Talk with your doctor if sadness keeps you from carrying on with your day-to-day life. Support may be necessary until you can manage the grief on your own.

What Can You Do?

In the beginning, you may find that taking care of details and keeping busy helps. For a while, family and friends may be around to assist you. But, there comes a time when you will have to face the change in your life.

Here are some things to keep in mind:

- **Take care of yourself.** Grief can be hard on your health. Exercise regularly, eat healthy food, and get enough sleep. Bad habits, such as drinking too much alcohol or smoking, can put your health at risk.

- **Try to eat right.** Some widowed people lose interest in cooking and eating. It may help to have lunch with friends. Sometimes eating at home alone feels too quiet. Turning on the radio or TV during meals can help. For information on nutrition and cooking for one, look for helpful books at your local library or bookstore, or online.

- **Talk with caring friends.** Let family and friends know when you want to talk about your spouse. They may be grieving too, and may welcome the chance to share memories. When possible, accept their offers of help and company.

- **Join a grief support group.** Sometimes, it helps to talk with people who also are grieving. Check with hospitals, religious communities, and local agencies to find out about support groups. Choose a support group where you feel comfortable sharing your feelings and concerns. Members of support groups often have helpful ideas or know of useful resources based on their own experiences. Online support groups make it possible to get help without leaving home.

- **Visit with members of your religious community.** Many people who are grieving find comfort in their faith. Praying, talking with others of your faith, reading religious or spiritual texts, or listening to uplifting music may also bring comfort.

- **Try not to make any major changes right away.** It's a good idea to wait for a while before making big decisions like moving or changing jobs.

- **See your doctor.** Keep up with your usual visits to your healthcare provider. If it has been a while, schedule a physical and bring your doctor up to date on any pre-existing medical conditions. Talk about any new health issues that may be of concern. Be sure to let your healthcare provider know if you are having trouble taking care of your everyday activities, like getting dressed or fixing meals.

- **Don't be afraid to seek professional help.** Sometimes, short-term talk therapy with a counselor can help.

- **Remember that your children are grieving, too.** It will take time for the whole family to adjust to life without your spouse. You may find that your relationship with your children and their relationships with each other have changed. Open, honest communication is important.

- **Mourning takes time.** It's common to have rollercoaster emotions for a while.

Does Everyone Feel the Same Way?

Men and women share many of the same feelings when a spouse dies. Both may deal with the pain of loss, and both may worry about the future. But, there also can be differences.

Many married couples divide up their household tasks. One person may pay bills and handle car repairs. The other person may cook meals and mow the lawn. Splitting up jobs often works well until there is only one person who has to do it all. Learning to manage new tasks—from chores to household repairs to finances—takes time, but it can be done.

Being alone can increase concerns about safety. It's a good idea to make sure there are working locks on the doors and windows. If you need help, ask your family or friends.

Facing the future without a husband or wife can be scary. Many men and women have never lived alone. Those who are both widowed and retired may feel very lonely and become depressed. Talk with your doctor about how you are feeling.

Take Charge of Your Life

After years of being part of a couple, it can be upsetting to be alone. Many people find it helps to have things to do every day. Whether you are still working or are retired, write down your weekly plans. You might:

- Take a walk with a friend.
- Visit the library.
- Volunteer.
- Try an exercise class.
- Join a singing group.
- Join a bowling league.
- Offer to watch your grandchildren.
- Consider adopting a pet.
- Take a class at a nearby senior center, college, or recreation center.
- Stay in touch with family and friends, either in person or online.

Is There More to Do?

When you feel stronger, you should think about getting your legal and financial affairs in order. You might need to:

- Write a new will and advance directive.

- Look into a durable power of attorney for legal matters and health care in case you are unable to make your own medical decisions in the future.

- Put joint property (such as a house or car) in your name.

- Check on changes you might need to make to your health insurance as well as your life, car, and homeowner's insurance.

- Sign up for Medicare by your 65th birthday.

- Make a list of bills you will need to pay in the next few months. For instance, State and Federal taxes, and your rent or mortgage.

When you are ready, go through your husband's or wife's clothes and other personal items. It may be hard to give away these belongings. Instead of parting with everything at once, you might make three piles: one to keep, one to give away, and one "not sure." Ask your children or others to help. Think about setting aside items like a special piece of clothing, watch, favorite book, or picture to give to your children or grandchildren as personal reminders of your spouse.

What about Going Out?

Having a social life on your own can be tough. It may be hard to think about going to parties or other social events by yourself. It can be hard to think about coming home alone. You may be anxious about dating. Many people miss the feeling of closeness that marriage brings. After a time, some are ready to have a social life again.

Here are some things to consider:

- Go at a comfortable pace. There's no rush.

- It's okay to make the first move when it comes to planning things to do.

- Try group activities. Invite friends for a potluck dinner or go to a senior center.

- With married friends, think about informal outings like walks, picnics, or movies rather than couple's events that remind you of the past.

- Find an activity you like. You may have fun and meet people who like to do the same thing.

- You can develop meaningful relationships with friends and family members of all ages.

- Many people find that pets provide important companionship.[29]

Divorce

Divorce means someone had the courage to say "enough." Surveys found women initiate 70% of divorces. So how do you exit a marriage that has so many moving parts, i.e., kids, friends, family, and finances? Well before you go running to the lawyers, you have to have a plan unless you are in danger. If you *are* in danger, contact The National Violence Hotline. Visit the website to find out more: http://www.thehotline.org/2015/05/abuse-and-mental-illne ss-is-there-a-connection/

Let's assume that you are not in danger, but you have been thinking about leaving for some time. If you have exhausted all the traditional options – counseling, individual therapy, church, date nights, and communication with your partner – and nothing has worked, here are some steps to take:

Step 1. Compile a pre- and post-budget. This will give you a clear understanding of the financial ramifications of this major event. Make sure you *understand* the numbers.

Step 2. Make sure you have adequate cash on hand and start working on Project Xero immediately. (Reread Chapter 5 Project Xero).

Step 3. If you don't have access to joint and family assets, find a way to get access. Don't assume you know everything about your spouse's assets.

Step 4. Contact your financial advisor or hire one to do an in-depth analysis of your financial viability post-divorce.

Step 5. Make sure you are comfortable with your personal and financial decision to leave.

Step 6. Can you afford the house? If not, where do you and the children want to live? This is a significant step because this will be your largest financial obligation.

Step 7. Get a referral to an attorney that specializes in divorce. I would recommend you try to have a collaborative divorce and use a mediator for negotiations of a divorce agreement.

Step 8. Be 120% confident that you gave it everything before you file for divorce. Have a conversation with your future ex-spouse, if possible. If not prepare emotionally for a rollercoaster ride. You will have to mentally and emotionally click on all cylinders because this could go on for some time. The cost of divorce will vary but the more combative, the more expensive it could become. Divorce is never easy, but if you are both mentally, emotionally, and financially ready, the process could go smoothly. Remove all your emotions and make all decisions based on fact.

Chapter 9

Cougaronomics

"Cougars are all the rage! I'm so glad that Hollywood and America are embracing women when they get in their 40s instead of putting us out to pasture."
— Vivica A. Fox

Cougaronomics: An experience for only the self-actualized woman that has the means and maturity to pursue a meaningful relationship with a partner much younger in spite of societal norms and traditional thinking.

This chapter is similar to Fifty Shades of Grey. It's a great fantasy, but doesn't apply to the broader population. If you are happily married, read this chapter, but understand that most of the information won't apply to your situation.

Cougaronomics only truly works for the self-actualized woman who has never married by choice, or been divorced or widowed. Cougaronomics is based on the foundational precepts of neuroeconomics and emotional intelligence. By the end of this chapter, you will have a better idea of the mindset needed to implement this concept entirely.

Family dynamics are shifting, and women's roles in money and finance are changing as well. Today, more women are either single or divorced than married.[30] When it comes to economic matters, the balance of power is shifting. Women outnumber men in the attainment of college and graduate degrees by 37%.[31] They are starting new businesses at twice the rate of men. Women comprise 43% of Americans with assets of $1.5 million or more; they own 40% of U.S. businesses. They are responsible for 83% of consumer purchases, 89% of U.S. bank accounts, and 51% of all personal wealth.[32] Fifty-Seven percent of women say they have more earning power than ever before. Almost two-thirds are the primary breadwinner in their family, and more than half see themselves as the Chief Financial Officer (CFO) of their household.[33]

To quote Beyoncé, "Women run the world."

Up until now, however, women have not translated that power into relationships on a massive scale. Cougaronomics leverages a woman's authority and freedom to do what men have done since the beginning of time. The facts are that women today are well positioned to rewrite the rules that were written by men. The question is: Can women who are winning in the boardroom take it all the way to the bank and beyond?

The findings, published in the journal *Evolution and Human Behavior*, disputes the "cougar" phenomenon popularized in TV shows and movies like "Cougar Town," starring Courteney Cox, and "Sex and the City" of women aged over 40 seeking "cubs." According to Dr. Michael Dunn of UWIC's Cardiff School of Health Sciences, who was the lead researcher of a study looking at age preferences of online dating men and women, Although there was some cultural variation in extremes, the results showed clearly that women across all age groups and cultures, targeted males either their own age or older."[34] Cougar myth busted.

Dr. Dunn went on to say, "A wide variety of evidence has shown that women when considering a potential long-term partner, focus more than males on cues indicative of wealth and status and these logically accumulate with age. Males conversely focus more intently on physical attractiveness cues, and these are correlated with the years of maximum fertility."[35]

"Women who understand Cougaronomics apply similar cues to their male counterparts, but also correlate physical ability and emotional support as key factors." Women outlive men by 5-10 years on average. Given this fact, if you are a woman having a male partner who is 5-15 years younger than you could be both financially prudent and mutually beneficial.[36]

Women face unique challenges in meeting their financial goals that men don't, including a longer life expectancy. Women spend more time in retirement, living 5 – 7 years longer than men, placing them at a greater risk of outliving their retirement assets, and increasing the chances of needing long-term care. Just 37% of people believe they will need long-term care but the reality is 70% will require it.[37] These issues can be dramatically different when applying Cougaronomics. A slight shift in thinking can increase your chances of living with a partner until death and in some cases, increase longevity and sexual compatibility.

So let's get into the logistics of Cougaronomics, which factors in pensions, health, dual income, sexual alignment, and much more. Let's compare two women who are both widowed at the age of 55. In scenario one, widow number one remarries a 62 year-old healthy male, while widow number two applies Cougaronomics and remarries a 47 year-old healthy male with less earned income. In the first case, the likelihood of the first widow playing a role in healthcare management increases dramatically. Taking advantage of a dual income would also have a smaller window. In the second case, the likelihood of widow two playing a role in healthcare management decreases and the opportunity for a longer dual income increases. In the second scenario, this widow would also have an opportunity to delay social security benefits because of having the dual income. Exploring this approach is simply something that could provide everyone involved with significant short-term and long-term benefits.

Women that use the Cougaronomics approach tend not to be effected by:

Fewer Years in the Workforce: Interrupting their careers to take care of family, women typically work 12 years less than men, receiving smaller social security benefits and only half the pension benefits that men receive.[38]

Having children: A study by PayScale and reported in Money found that a married, childless woman received 31.1% more salary than a married woman with children.[39]

Today, women still earn just 78¢ for every dollar that a man earns, African American women, 64¢, Hispanic women just 56¢. And social security is especially important to women, yet more than four out of five women take social security early, locking in lower payments for life and missing out on potentially hundreds of thousands of dollars in retirement income, and it's no different for widows or divorcees. Forty-eight percent of women getting divorced or separated and 50% of women who have become widows said these two events created a financial crisis in their lives and made them realize the importance of becoming financially aware and independent. For widows, the average age of widow-hood is just 59, with 1/3 losing their spouse before age 45. Only 8% of widows between 55 and 64 will remarry; after 65 it's just 2%. Eighty percent of men die married, while 80% of women die single.

For divorcees, a woman typically sees a considerable reduction in her standard of living after divorce while her ex-husband enjoys an increase in his. The fact is, due to the death of a spouse or divorce, 90% of women will be solely responsible for their finances at some point in their lives. Whether you are single, married, widowed, or divorced, financial success for women starts with education followed by action.

When asked what financial advice women would pass on to their daughters or granddaughters, the top answer given: "Don't depend on others for your financial security."

A man is not a retirement plan, but under the Cougaronomic strategy, he can be a launching pad for the new chapter in your life. As women take more responsibility for their finances, here is a checklist to see if this approach is really for you:

Checklist

1. I'm self-confident in who I am and not easily influenced by social norms or friends/family. That's me or not me.

2. I'm looking for companionship and flexibility without the baggage of a traditional relationship. That's me or not me.

3. I believe that I'm strong enough emotionally to accept public gawking, gossip, and the occasional conflict because of the age gap. That's me or not me.

4. I'm often told that I look much younger than my actual age. That's me or not me.

5. I find myself disappointed in the energy and conversation of men my age. That's me or not me.

6. I'm okay with being the financially responsible partner for most expenses attached to the relationship. That's me or not me.

7. I feel confident in my ability to socialize in any setting. That's me or not me.

8. I work out at least three days per week. That's me or not me.

9. I enjoy spending time with myself, but would like to be with someone when traveling, dining, and participating in general activities. I believe in living life to the max. That's me or not me.

10. I 'm adventurous and open to trying new things. That's me or not me.

You should consider this approach if you answered eight or more questions with "That's me."

You can sign up for a complimentary introduction workshop on Cougaronomics at www.holisticplanners.com. I address all of the unique challenges women face when it comes to finding a mate and reaching their true personal and financial well-being.

I provide a personalized blueprint created just for you. After all, this is your life. It's your future. You have worked hard for this; you have earned it! Why not maximize your relationship and finances now so that you can get the most from your retirement savings later?

"There are older men with younger women but you don't see a lot of older women with younger men. There are some women who have been able to do it but not often."
— Tori Amos

Chapter 10

Viagraville

"Life is really simple, but we insist on making it complicated."
— Confucius

Viagraville is defined as the town where the ego controls the day and legacies are often destroyed. In the age of the media-driven agenda to promote youth and manhood through status or sex, this can be a very dangerous place to visit or live. How do so many men find themselves passing through this town or worse yet staying? This town on the surface seems so attractive, and sometimes unavoidable, to most men. Consider that this is one detour that can ruin your financial future, destroy your family, or leave you alone wondering how you've lost it all trying to recapture the un-recapturable.

Throughout this chapter, we will offer examples, mindsets, and facts to consider before you visit.

The most common reason most visit Viagraville is to recapture a stage of life that they believe they missed. Some may have sacrificed their 20's and 30's building a career or were in a marriage that didn't work. New social norms can also play a factor in how you see yourself or life in general. By most accounts, these things can never be recreated to a level of meaningful satisfaction. In the book *Think and Grow Rich,* Napoleon Hill published in 1937 and still relevant in 2017, writes about mastering sex transmutation. He writes there is no other road to Genius than through willful self-effort. A man may attain great heights of financial or business achievement, solely by the driving force of sex energy, but history is filled with evidence that he may, and usually does, carry with him certain traits of character, which rob him of the ability to either hold or enjoy his fortune.[40] It is up to us to understand which phase of life we are in and leverage the knowledge that we have due to life experience.

The question is, how do I properly use this energy or essence of power to gain the life I so much want to have? This sex energy can be best maximized in the early and late stages of life. Between ages 20-40 you are trying to establish and prove your manhood, and beyond 40 you are in a struggle or fight to maintain your manhood. The most costly and impactful of both phases are the time and money spent on things that don't have a lasting impact. In the first phase of life, sex transmutation can be beneficial because of all the energy you have, which can be channeled into your personal and financial wellness. Focus on relationships and results early in life, and the next phase will take care of itself, including the mate, money, and material items that you think are important. In the second phase, sex transmutation can be beneficial because all the wisdom you've gained should replace your youthful energy. You should take the opportunity to maximize your earning potential and spend time with those that matter. The question remains: Will you take this stage of life and maximize it or squander it once again?

Napoleon Hill talks about the importance of the application of his most important success principles of Sex Transmutation to turn up the energy in a proper manner to access the creative energy within.[41] A millionaire once stated when asked how did you do it "forget the girls and focus on one woman, and she'll help you achieve everything." So now that the foundation has been established let's take a look at the progression of life as a man seeking to become personally and financially relevant.

The first thing you will realize when you arrive in Viagraville is that everything costs more than you remembered and you don't have the energy to do most of the things that are available. It is important to keep in mind that in most cases men don't ever lose their desire, just the ability. Women lose the desire, not the ability. So now that you have come to this significant truth, you are ready to consider factors that will impact your life and legacy forever.

The cost of starting over or being alone in your last phase of life can affect your health, wealth, and legacy. For Baby Boomers, divorce has almost become, like marriage, a rite of passage. The post-World War II generation is setting new records for divorce: Americans over 50 are twice as likely to get divorced as people of that age were 20 years ago. For most men, but not all, it's about sex. For most women, it's about companionship. So the divide continues, and we must decide how to navigate this phase of life if we plan to stay in Viagraville.

In Viagraville, the standard has been set – get a young wife and start a new family with or without kids. Take for example Richard Williams, the father of Venus and Serena, having a baby in his 70's with his 33 year-old wife.*Recently filed for divorce! Not all of you will have the resources of Mr. Williams, so don't think this is something the average man should pursue. This example is just one example of what happens in Viagraville.

While some studies show that men end up wealthier after divorce on average, it is also proven that men suffer from higher rates of suicide after divorce. They are also more prone to alcoholism, weight gain, and mental health issues.

179

If a new wife or young companion won't do it for you, Viagraville has many other options. How about purchasing that "THING"? You fill in the blank. However, "that thing" is often a depreciating asset and the enthusiastic feeling is short lived. Now if it's not the new wife, young companion, or "that thing," what could it be? Viagraville, just like New York or Vegas, never sleeps. You will find yourself doing seemingly harmless activities that will not appear important until you realize this isn't the first phase but the last.

Now let's talk about legacy. In Viagraville, the loss of legacy most often occurs at the expense of what in all accounts would have been a great life. One recent example is Bill O'Reilly. Mr. O'Reilly had it all but still chose to visit Viagraville because of what I believe to be the ultimate power: SEX. Now the once-biggest star on a network is without the one thing that gave him relevance – a platform to display his opinion. No one ever leaves Viagraville without some sign that they visited.

Now that you know that Viagraville isn't as attractive as it once seemed, you have a decision to make. Most will still visit, but my hope is that most won't stay! Staying relevant can only be obtained by controlling the things you can control. The only thing you can control is you.

These are some facts to consider if it's necessary to visit:

- Research suggests that men who get and stay married live almost ten years longer than their unmarried peers.

- Married men earn 10-40% more income.

- Men who get and stay married are in much better financial shape than their peers who divorced or never married.

- The typical 50-something married guy has three times the assets of his unmarried peer, about $167,000 to $49,000.[42] So it's costly to visit Viagraville at this stage.

- A National health and social life survey finds that 51% of married men are emotionally satisfied with sex, compared to 39% of cohabiting men and 36% of single men.[43]

- Married men have better mental and physical health.

- Elders who have a good marriage have significantly less depression, better mood, and life satisfaction.[44]

When you see the exit for Viagraville, please press the gas. Your life and legacy depend on it. This phase of sex transmutation can pay the biggest dividends. Stay relevant by taking that desire and channeling it toward a new business, reestablishing relationships, or finally discovering your purpose or passion.

"There are two great days in a person's life - the day we are born and the day we discover why."
— William Barclay

Chapter 11

Casino Capitalism

"The Western financial system is rapidly coming to resemble
nothing as much as a vast casino."
—Susan Strange, British Economist

If your brain is wired for risk-taking and our stock market is a casino, how do you make sure you're not gambling your savings away? We want to believe that the stock market is rational. Logically, stocks should go up when profits are being made and down when profits dive. Unfortunately, it's not as straightforward as that. With less government regulation it's becoming even harder to make a good bet on the stock market. So what's a small investor saving for retirement to do? Not betting is a good start. Here are some strategies that can help:

Dollar Cost Averaging: Sounds complicated, but it's not. Dollar Cost Averaging is investing in an investment vehicle, such as a stock, with a fixed dollar amount at regular time intervals, be it weekly, monthly, or quarterly. This strict regimen takes the emotion out of buying stocks because you will be investing without consideration of stock price. Also, the set amount will result in you buying more stock shares when the price is down and less when the price is high.

When the stock is down, you'll be getting a bargain and will reap the rewards when the price is high. Sort of like finding a great book on sale and discovering it's worth much more down the road.

Index Fund: An index fund is a mutual fund or exchange-traded fund (ETF) designed to follow certain preset rules so that the fund can track a specified basket of underlying investments. Index Funds are low cost and are a passive investment. You don't need to make a lot of decisions. As an article from Forbes noted Index Funds are the "low-cost, passive strategy and provide the highest probability of reaching your financial goals.[45]

Automatic Saving Deposits: Setting up an automatic saving deposit directly to your retirement savings takes the emotion out of saving. With automatic savings, you also won't forget to save, or procrastinate.

Microsavings: This works well for anyone, but particularly doctors or business owners who deal with large amounts of cash daily. The objective is to get the money out of your spending account and into a saving account where it is not readily available. This avoids the trap of spending these funds before you can invest them.

Investing in you: Investing in yourself will be the most important thing you can do to become rich faster and sooner, by far. Why? Because you are giving yourself what the market or an outside force cannot take away. This common myth is that you need more money, but in reality, you need to invest more in yourself to become the best version of you.

Today's retirees in all likelihood need to find other sources of income other than their savings and social security. Just fifty years ago, financing retirement was a significantly different ballgame. Back then people tended to work for the same company for many years, and many businesses had pension plans for employees. Also, people didn't live as long as they do today. So today's generation needs to find a new way to retire. You can't afford to gamble with future retirement because of old approaches and mindsets.

Saving: Is it enough?

The only way to finance retirement today is to save more and spend less. That's not easy. Today's retiree depends on 401(k) saving plans, other savings, and Social Security. We're living longer so financing retirement could be a 30-year proposition. Do the math. For the average middle class family with kids, it's just about impossible to save and curtail spending enough to gather a significant amount of money to last a full retirement. Even for Millennials, with huge tuition loans and skyrocketing housing costs, saving for retirement can get dicey. That means in all probability you may need to find some way to bring in income during retirement.

A Pew Research survey conducted in September 2011 showed that 49% of respondents ages 35 to 44 were concerned about retirement finances, compared with 41% of 45-54 year-olds and 37% of those ages 55-64. The majority of people who said they would work into their 70s would do so because they needed the additional income, not because they loved their job.[46]

It's important to save even if it will never be enough for your full retirement. Any savings you have will be a critical nest egg for maintaining a desired lifestyle. The flip side of saving, however, is spending less before you retire so you can save and not be in debt when you do retire. This doesn't mean you have to be a miser all your life, but it does mean that you need to evaluate what is important to you and what is just an extravagance that you really can't afford.

Is a monster house needed to house four kids and two adults? Do you need to send your kids to private schools (which frequently cost as much as a college education) or are the public schools in your neighborhood just as good? Do you need the most expensive car to get you safely from Point A to Point B? These are the types of questions you need to ask yourself before you retire.

Chapter 12

Ready or Not

"Only I can change my life. No one can do it for me."
— Carol Burnett

Most people use the word "tomorrow" as if it is promised, but in reality, we only have today.

You may have said, "I'll start planning for retirement tomorrow, or someday," but neither of those time frames is as powerful as today. This chapter is about planning for the future and taking action today. "The amazing thing I've seen in life," one recently retired woman told me, "You always know when it's time to retire, but you often question if you are ready."

Retirees don't come fully prepared for retirement. In fact, retirement is about continuous preparation. Getting ready for retirement does not happen overnight; it's a series of small steps that get you to your goal. It's tempting to think "small" is insignificant; only "a lot" matters. However, transitions and changes in life frequently start with small steps. What's important in life often starts with changes that are small and slow. Important changes don't always come with fanfare and bright lights.

For a new retiree, moving through the preparation for retirement may be a little like flying in an airplane during a storm: Flying through turbulence, the plane gyrates, but eventually, the plane breaks through to clear skies. You may be anxious and uncertain, but with a well-planned retirement process, you will land just fine. You can weather most any storm and ultimately emerge stronger from the experience when you have a plan in place.

Retiring also includes setting expectations. Providing a framework doesn't take away your freedom. In fact, planning helps you do the things you want to do without worry. Preparation is like your safety net in case of unexpected turbulence.

Rebranding yourself

Being retired appears to be complex, but it can be simplified if planned properly. Planning involves taking the time to reflect on who you are and what you want in this next stage of life.

I once received a note from a client who wrote: "Demetrius, I wish I were like my friends who want to retire, travel, and be socially active. But that just isn't my personality." All retirees must accept themselves for who they are and not what others say they should be. You may like to play bridge, tennis, or travel. Or a perfect day for you, may be finding a comfy chair and reading that novel you've heard about. Doing what makes you happy is a far more meaningful gift to yourself than trying to replicate what others think retirement should be. And what's more, this is the time when you can live the life you want. The last thing in the world you have to do is pretend.

As you near retirement and start planning for the years ahead, you can't control every aspect of forthcoming events. It may be painful to see yourself modifying or even rejecting activities you once did with ease and adopting interests that you never considered before. But out of that process may come the discovery of what aligns with your life's purpose now. Becoming comfortable with the new you will allow you to enjoy this chapter of your life even more.

You can thank the Boomer generation for changing the perception of what is old. Sixty is the new forty is not just a catchy saying. Sitting in a rocking chair watching TV is not the goal of most retiring Boomers. A Chase 2016 Generational Money Talks study found that Boomers are looking to be active and planning to spend money on experiences, not things.

In other words, Boomers just want to have fun, which isn't such a bad goal. The word elderly seems to be going the way of the dodo bird as well. "Elderly" is rarely used when referring to retirees, even when they are in their 80s. [47]

As you near retirement, look for the clues as to whether or not you are ready. Your gut will let you know when it's time. As you do an analysis of your emotional and financial readiness, little by little, you will find yourself with less and less stress around the transition.

Planning is not only financial. You need to discover what you want to do in retirement. How will you spend your days? How will you continue to be relevant to yourself and others? Even when you have done the work to get ready, there will be times when you may feel the world has turned upside down. Holding on to the knowledge that you have a strategy to create a life filled with activities that matter to you will get you through the tough times. Like the client, I mentioned earlier who didn't want to travel or be socially active in retirement because it just wasn't him, you need to be true to yourself and who you are.

Those who have adjusted well to retirement have learned to feel valued and appreciated, and to remind themselves that the tough times do pass.

Today's retirees are very lucky. With advanced technology and studies on how to stay healthy, we are living longer and remaining active longer than our parents ever thought possible. According to an AgeWave study, U.S. Boomers are significantly more proactive than previous generations when it comes to health.[48] It is they that drove the fitness movement. Before the Boomer generation, less than a quarter of adults did any form of exercise. By 1980, six out of ten adults exercised on a regular basis.[49]

Now that people are living longer, saving and minimizing expenses becomes even more important in the Golden Years. We all know individuals who have retired and wished they had saved more, used less to live, or had opened a 401(k) sooner. I've often noticed that when someone feels that way, that person doesn't feel great about his or her choices. I think that's where it all begins for me as an advisor. I try to help clients accept their choices so they can be open to available options. When I assist them in recognizing where they are now, I can help them build the foundation for a successful retirement.

Knowing that support is both needed and available when you are nearing retirement makes it easier for you to make that final decision. I have come to realize how important the planning process is to our clients for developing confidence and creativity. Sometimes working with a client at an early stage in the process of retirement, we may find that resources are limited. Therefore, some of their plans may be limited as well. We work together to find alternatives, and we often find better outcomes than the original plan anticipated.

Retirement Anxiety

When facing a situation that frightens us, we often overreact or react too late. Procrastination is rarely, if ever, beneficial. Procrastination is only good for creating anxiety. So if you are a procrastinator, remember that you'll be more stressed if you put things off rather than diving right in.

Concerns around retirement occur in many different variations, but most commonly it centers on the fear of outliving the money! The Motley Fool reported on the findings of a study by the American Institute of CPAs that 57% of financial advisors found their client's primary worry was running out of money.[50]

Other fears or stresses may involve selling a primary residence that's been owned for thirty years or more, or leaving family and friends for a warmer climate. People manage these scenarios in different ways; some go it alone, some talk with friends and family; some hire a financial advisor.

The resources in the back of this book are centered on providing you with the tools you'll need to minimize these retirement concerns and allow you to navigate your way through a world where retirement no longer exists.

Tools and Worksheets:
Ready or Not

Download a full-sized copy of these resources at:

www.holisticplanners.com

REDEFINING YOU

This is a guide to help you look before you leap. It is said that there is a tendency for most men to measure themselves by what they do and for most women to measure themselves by who they serve. Completing this exercise will allow you to marry both viewpoints. This isn't about what others may or may not measure. This is about you. Holistic you.

Before your parents, job/title, friends/ colleagues, or the world defined you, how did you see yourself? (one sentence)	
List the most common terms people use to describe you:	

List your unique skills:	
What impact can you make in your community that will give your life meaning or change someone else's life?	
List your passions or hobbies that can be shared with others:	

Staying relevant requires that you to redefine how you were known so that you can be remembered. Take the time to understand your unique skills as well as your power to redefine yourself.

Life is about service. Be of service to yourself by redefining yourself. Remove the barriers that surround and stamp down your unique skills and gifts. It's time to practice, develop, and share them in service to others.

"I've learned that people will forget what you said, people will forget what you did, but people will never forget how you made them feel."
— Maya Angelou

Retirement Statistics	Data
Average retirement age	63
Average length of retirement	18 years
Average savings of a 50 year old	$42,797
Average net worth of a 55-64 year old	$45,447
Total cost for a couple over 65 to pay for medical treatment over a 20 year span	$218,000
Percentage of people ages 30-54 who believe they will not have enough money put away for retirement	80%
Percentage of Americans over 65 who rely completely on Social Security	36%
Percentage of Americans who don't save anything for retirement	38%
Number of Americans who turn 65 per day	6,100

Percentage of population that is 65 years of age or older	13%
Out of 100 people who starts working at the age of 25, by the age 65:	
Will be considered wealthy	1%
Have adequate capital stowed away for retirement	4%
Will still be working	3%
Are dependent on Social Security, friends, relatives or charity	63%
Are dead	29%
Americans older than 50 account for:	
Percent of all financial assets	77%
Percent of total consumer demand	54%
Prescription drug purchases	77%
All over-the-counter drugs	61%
Auto Sales	47%
All luxury travel purchases	80%

AMOUNT NEEDED IN SAVINGS FOR RETIREMENT		
Monthly income need	Savings Needed for 20 Years	Savings Needed for 30 Years
$1,000	$166,696	$212,150
$2,000	$333,392	$424,300
$3,000	$500,087	$636,450
$4,000	$666,783	$848,601
$5,000	$833,479	$1,060,751
$6,000	$1,000,175	$1,272,901
$7,000	$1,166,871	$1,485,051
$8,000	$1,333,567	$1,697,201
$9,000	$1,500,262	$1,909,351
$10,000	$1,666,958	$2,121,501

The above sums assume your portfolio will earn a 6 percent annualized return during the course of your retirement and endure 2 percent annual inflation erosion.

Statistic Sources & References
Sources: U.S. Census Bureau, Saperston Companies, Bankrate

Content Author: Statistic Brain
Date research was conducted: January 3, 2016
Retirement Statistics
Financial

HOW DO YOU COMPARE?

Age Range	Median Net Worth	Average Net Worth
Less than 35	$14,200	$73,500
35 – 44	$69,400	$299,200
45 – 54	$144,700	$542,700
55 – 64	$248,700	$843,800
65 – 74	$190,100	$690,900
75 or more	$163,100	$528,100

Sources: U.S. Federal Reserve

Credit Score Statistics	Data
National average credit score (FICO 300 – 850)	691
National average credit score (VantageScore 501 – 990)	749
Percent of people who have obtained a copy of their credit report	39%
Percent who have checked their credit within the past 12 months	35%
Percent of American adults who admit they do not know their credit score	37%
Percent of undergraduate college students who	2%

have no credit history	
Average number of credit obligations each consumer has on record at a credit bureau	13
Average length of a consumers oldest credit obligation	14 years
Percent of consumers who have a credit history shorter than 5 years	5%

Credit Score Factors	% Factor
Payment history, late payments	35 %
Credit utilization, ratio of current revolving debt	30 %
Length of credit history	15 %
Types of credit used, installment, revolving, consumer finance, mortgage	10 %
Recent credit inquiries	10 %

Average Credit Score By Age (FICO)	Data
18 – 24	643
25 – 34	651

35 – 44	644
45 – 54	660
55 +	693

States with the highest average credit score (FICO)	Avg Score
Wisconsin	681
Hawaii	681
Massachusetts	677
New Jersey	676
Minnesota	674
Washington	671
Connecticut	671
New York	669
Vermont	668
Colorado	664
New Hampshire	663

States with the lowest average credit score (FICO)	Avg Score
Mississippi	618
Louisiana	625
Arkansas	628
Alabama	629
South Carolina	629
Kentucky	632
West Virginia	633
Nevada	638
South Carolina	639
Texas	639
Indiana	642

Source: Statistic Brain Research Institute (Online / Direct Response Mail)

NEED FOR LIFE INSURANCE

*EACH PERSON OR FAMILY IS DIFFERENT

MY OPINION

Through my experience and research, I would suggest that everyone should obtain 1 million dollars of coverage for each person in the household. So a family of four should have 4 million dollars of coverage on both the mother and father.

Here are the facts: 44 percent of U.S. households had individual life insurance as of 2010 — a 50-year low. In 1960, 72 percent of Americans owned individual life insurance. In 1992, 55 percent owned it. (Source: LIMRA's Trends in Life Insurance Ownership study).

I believe this has a direct link to happiness in a marriage. Purchasing life insurance is the greatest act of love. You are say that I love you so much that even in my absence I want you to live the same lifestyle that you are accustomed to. See the worksheet to determine how much coverage you should have.

My opinion: Buying term and investing the difference DOESN'T WORK. Only 2 percent of term policies pay a death benefit. It simply doesn't work because people don't save the difference. My opinion is that you need some combination of permanent and term insurance to protect your business or family. The goal is to cover your need either forever or temporarily. See a quick spreadsheet to assess your insurance needs.

INCOME	TOTAL	NOTE
1. Total annual income your family would need if you died today	$_____	(Ideally between 70%-80%)
2. Annual income your family would receive from other sources	$_____	For example, spouse's earning or a fixed pension.(Do not include income earned on your assets, as it is addressed later in calculation.)
3. Income to be replaced	$_____	Subtract line 2 from line 1
4. Capital need for income	$_____	Multiply line 3 by general run of thumb 10

EXPENSES

5. Funeral and other final expenses	$_____	Ideally the greater of$15,000 or 4% of your estate

6. Mortgage and other outstanding debts

$_____

Include mortgage balance, credit card balance, car loans, etc

7. Capital need for college

$_____

**Private $181,480 ; Public $80,360 ballpark Cost X # Kids

8. Total capital required

$_____

Add items 4,5,6,7

9. Savings and investment

$_____

Bank accounts, money market, cd, stocks, bonds, mutual funds, annuities, etc.

10. Retirement savings:

$_____

IRAs,401ks,SEP plans, Simple IRA plan Keoghs, pension and profit sharing plans***

11. Present amount of life insurance

$_____

Include group insurance as well as insurance purchased on you own

12. Total income $_____   Add lines 9,10 and
producing assets   11

13. Life insurance $_____   Subtract line 12
needed   from 8

Chapter 13

Retirement Roadblocks

"Sometimes the questions are complicated, and the answers are simple."
— Dr. Seuss

You will face four major roadblocks that are just as challenging as the obstacles that faced your parents: Student loans, high cost of home-ownership, Super Parent Syndrome, and the Sandwich Effect.

Retirement Roadblocks: 45 and Under

In the Project Xero chapter, we talked about paying off debt and leveraging those dollars. The one exception is student loans, which I believe should be the last item you pay off. It's the only good debt you have if you are utilizing your degree to its maximum potential. Also, the average student loan rate is 5.7% versus19.99% on credit cards and most revolving credit.

Undergraduate and graduate debt by degree:[51]

DEGREE	COMPENSATION	% OF GRADUATES
MBA	$42,000	11%
Master of Education	$50,879	16%
Master of Science	$50,400	8%
Law	$140,616	4%
Medicine and Health Sciences	$161,772	5%

MBA = $42,000 (11% of graduate degrees)

Master of Education = $50,879 (16% of graduate degrees)

Master of Science = $50,400 (18%)

Master of Arts = $58,539 (8%)

Law = $140,616 (4%)

Medicine and health sciences = $161,772 (5%)[52]

As these student loan debt statistics show, the cost of attending college is becoming a growing burden for a huge portion of Americans.

You will find it difficult to implement Project Xero if you focus too much on paying off student loans.

The wiser option is to look for employment with loan forgiveness if you don't have to sign up for a long-term commitment or lower than market rate salary. To compromise your income for loan forgiveness may or may not be worthwhile.

High Cost of Homeownership

Homeownership is directly correlated with future wealth. Home prices are at record highs. The national median home price (NAR) has grown by 34% over the last four years, while hourly wages have increased just 10% in the same period.[53] This, in turn, delays the opportunity to build equity and take advantage of communities with quality education options.

Homeownership declined among those aged 35 to 44 from 67% in 2007 to 58% in 2015. That's the largest decline among all age groups. According to Susan Wachter, Professor of Real Estate and Finance at The Wharton School of the University of Pennsylvania, this group was hit the hardest due to slowing wage growth and foreclosures.

Renters occupied about 36.3% of households last year, the highest figure in a decade, according to a new Census Bureau report. At the same time, homeownership dropped to 63.6% compared to 69% ten years ago.[54] The solution will require out-of-the-box thinking and non-traditional strategies.

One out-of-the-box concept is the Investment Club:

This strategy is simple enough to implement. Create an investment club with five people and live together for the six years a typical new homebuyer in his or her early 30's would spend renting before making his first home purchase. According to the real estate data firm, Zillow, this is up from 2.6 years in the 1970's.[55]

Each person is responsible for coming up with 20% of the down payment on a fixer-upper or apartment building in an emerging part of the city.

The scenario looks something like this:

- Step 1: A legal document is drafted and approved by all members.

- Step 2: A brokerage account is established for the down payment.

- Step 3: Each member deposits a monthly amount into the brokerage account until the down payment goal is reached.

- Step 4: Engage a real estate professional for potential properties.

- Step 5: The group closes on the first property.

- Step 6: Because each is paying only 1/5 of the mortgage, each will have a surplus income.

- Step 7: Repeat, using the surplus for shared living expenses and deposit the necessary amount in a brokerage account.

- Step 8: Member 1 closes on the property and recruits someone else to replace him or her in the club.

- Step 9: Repeat until all founding members have purchased homes.

There are many moving parts to this approach, but if you match personalities and financial capacity, this could be a win-win. This is not a new concept, but one that has been around for many years. This concept can also work for generational cohabitation, which includes grandchildren, and parents living in a larger and more upscale community.

Retirement Roadblocks: (30 to 50 years old)

There are retirement roadblocks facing individuals today because of outdated approaches and beliefs. We will address them with both examples and statistical facts.

Super Parent Syndrome

The main roadblock between you and a comfortable retirement is your children.[56] If you don't have kids, you have a significant head start in creating wealth. Now, you maybe thinking, how can my precious children impact my retirement. Before I begin, let me say that children are one of the greatest gifts that one could be given. So let me explain.

People either undervalue education (the poor), overvalue private education (the middle and upper middle class), or have access to or have been taught how to leverage education (the rich or wealthy). How you view education is important because it will impact how much you can save for retirement and college.[57]

Let's focus on the middle and upper classes. Many middle class families decide to provide their children with an elementary through high school private education out of necessity or personal preference.

The middle class does not receive any outside financial support to do so. They are left in an awkward position when compared to upper middle class or well-resourced parents.

In the following example, we look at the numbers: Middle class parents are paying private school tuition out of cash flow which leads to less saving for retirement or emergency reserves. Upper middle class or better-resourced families pay tuition from surplus monthly income, inheritance, or grandparents. Let's just see how much it would cost a middle class family in retirement assets: $30,000 per year may total as much as $1,121,369 before taxes and inflation.

This assumes you have a tax-deferred investment with a rate of return of 7% that compounds annually. Let's also assume that all new contributions are made at the end of each yearly period. If your investment earnings were taxable at a combined marginal tax rate of 29.5%, your ending balance would be reduced to $910,270. After taxes and 2.9% annually for inflation, your total would be further reduced to $528,784.

Aside from this education cost, families spend approximately $245,000 to raise the average child to 18 years of age.[58] Then comes college with a potential bill of $100,000 for a public college. An elite private college will be much more. This is only for one child. What if you have two or more children!

The chart below shows how sending your children to private school could jeopardize your retirement, depending on your economic class.

	UNDER RESOURCED (POOR)	MIDDLE CLASS	WELL RESOURCED (RICH+)
Tuition*	No Major Impact	Major Impact	No Major Impact
Tuition Funded by*	Financial Aid	Cash Flow/Income	Surplus income / Assets Dividends/ Grandparents
Scholarships/ Aid	Many	Very little / None	N/A
Wealth Accumulation for Parents*	No Impact	Major Impact* Lost or minimized investment opportunity for the future*tuition invested for one child is about $1.3 million with considering college	No Impact
Socialization	Major Impact *80/20 positive and negative	Moderate Impact *90/10 positive and negative	No Impact

Average Distance	10-45 miles Moderate Impact	5-35 miles Moderate Impact	5-30 miles *Third Party or Spouse No Impact
Travel Time	1-1 ½ hour Moderate Impact	30-55 minutes Moderate Impact	No Impact 30-45 minutes* Nanny or Third Party support
School Events / Donations	No Impact	Moderate Impact	No Impact
Quality of Education	Major Impact	Moderate Impact	Moderate / No Impact

*Disclaimer these are general assumptions and not intended to be a complete view of the impact or non-impact on non-traditional**free education options.*

There are many reasons to send your child to a private school, but most middle class families have mortgaged their future in exchange for educating their child today. Obviously, you want to provide your child or children with the best opportunities to succeed, but at what cost? The biggest investment that should be made on your child is parenting, i.e., quality, reading aloud and often, life/travel exposure, and love. Please don't get me wrong, you should never discount the power of education. Most studies indicate that early childhood is a key indicator of future success. Note: Parenting and Grit are something that is often overlooked and can't ever be truly measured.

Options to Lessen the Impact

- Earn more money
- Move to a community that has great public schools.
- Go public after 3rd grade or 8th grade, or do the inverse and go private after 8th grade
- Dual Income for tuition offset
- Hope that your child becomes _____ so he/she can take care of you in retirement. (funniest line in the book)
- Put your head in the sand and just see how things turn out.

Memo to the middle class

If you can both save for retirement and send your child to private school, you should do it. If you are going to experience the need to talk about how much you pay, or cut back on pleasurable activities, you should not. You should not look at a school for status or networking. If you aren't in those circles already, it would be very rare for you to retain those relationships after your child's education is over.

So the bottom line is: you shouldn't mortgage your future if you can't afford it. We all want to be beautiful, skinny/in shape, and rich, but if it were easy, we wouldn't have an epidemic of obesity, poverty, or a reason for a rapidly growing medicated (that includes weed/prescription drugs) society. Wake up and teach your kids about love, entrepreneurship, saving and investing, and lifelong learning.

Life Income Projections

"Taking jobs to build up your resume is like saving up sex for old age."
Warren Buffet

Specialize degree, i.e., medicine, law, and engineering	Highest earning potential of $4.4 million
Doctoral degree	Earns an average of $3.4 million
Master's degree	Earns an average of Earns an average of $2.5%
Bachelor's degree	Earns an average of $2.1%
High diploma	Earns an average of $1.2 million

These figures are based on 1999 earnings projected over a typical work life, defined by the Census Bureau as the period from ages 25 through 64.

"While many people stop working at an age other than 65, or start before age 25, this range of 40 years provides a practical benchmark for many people," noted the Census Bureau.

Sandwich Generation

According to the Pew Research Center, "nearly half (47% of adults in their 40s and 50s have a parent age 65 or older and are either raising a young child or financially supporting a grown child (age 18 or older).[59] If you're female, the statistics are even bleaker. According to Caregiver Statistics, "the typical caregiver is a 49 year-old woman caring for her widowed 69 year-old mother. The female caregiver is also married and employed. More than 37 percent have children living with them.[60]

This means there are a lot of Baby Boomers, particularly women, who are pitching in to help their parents with daily tasks, such as cooking, cleaning, and transportation, at the same time they are taking care of their children, whether toddlers or adults. So, it's no surprise that this Sandwich Generation is scrambling to figure out the best combination of pitching in and tapping outside help. Intergeneration caregiving is also hurting financially. The Pew study found that "roughly 48% of adults ages 40-59 have provided some financial support to at least one grown child in the past year."[61]

If you are one of these people caught in the middle, the first step is to assess the situation, say experts – ideally, before it becomes urgent. "You need first to have a family meeting," says Chad Terry, director of investment and retirement education at BlackRock.[62] He suggests discussing any housing issues. Is he or she able to live without help? If so, then perhaps you could consider downsizing the elder's residence. Often, elders own their homes outright, and can clear $300,000 to $500,000 from a home sale—enough to buy a condo and have money left over to provide supplemental care. Another option to consider is relocating to a state with lower taxes on retirement income.

An even more strategic step is to think about looking for states with a lower cost of long-term care. Extreme? Consider that 70% of 65 year-olds can expect to use some form of long-term care during their lives, according to the U.S. Department of Health and Human Services (HHS). The nationwide median annual cost of a home health aide is over $46,000, while adult day care can be more than $17,000, according to most recent studies.

What if the elder can't live without assistance? The least expensive option may be in-home care where family members help with caregiving needs. "Family members pitching in can help make ends meet, but such care has its own costs. The caregiver loses money from time away from work," says Terry,[63] which could lead to fewer promotions or advancement in wages, thus jeopardizing the caregiver's retirement.

If these options don't provide enough care, the next level is generally assisted-living facilities or skilled-nursing facilities. The cost of assisted living facilities and nursing homes has recently climbed by 4%—much more sharply than the 1% hike in the cost of in-home care, according to Nationwide research, the annual cost of a private room in a nursing home averages $87,600, while a one bedroom, single occupancy in an assisted living facility costs $42,000.[64]

These healthcare costs need not be out-of-pocket. There are a variety of long-term-care insurance programs, riders for life insurance, and other financial vehicles to help offset the costs of healthcare not covered by an employer's healthcare plan or Medicare. "Most people pick this up [long-term care insurance] when they're in their 50s, and hope they're not going to use them for a decade or two," Terry says. "You can't get them [long-term insurance] once you need them." Ideally, those kinds of conversations should also happen at the family meeting.[65]

Jobs After Education

If you think your child will become the next great athlete on scholarship to a high-cost university, don't hold your breath.

Fun Fact 1: From 2004 census statistics of the US Labor Department and the American Medical Association, there are approximately 885,000 (884,974) doctors in the US. This represents about 0.29% of the population or one-third of 1%.[66]

There is roughly one doctor to 300 people in the U.S. Races other than Caucasians are significantly underrepresented. Caucasians represent 47.8% of all physicians. Black doctors only make up 2.3%, and Hispanics about 3.2%. The largest minority percentage is Asians, at 8.3% of all doctors.

There are more than 480,000 NCAA student-athletes, and fewer than two percent will go pro in their sports.[67]

Fun Fact 3: Your kid becoming CEO at a Fortune 500 probably won't happen either. 404,000 and .8% chance if you're a minority. 4% if you a woman. 9% in general.

I'm full of optimism, so you or your child could be the one. With enough positive self-talk, no self-sabotage, and unique group skills, your percentage goes up dramatically. The most reliable way to stay relevant both financially and personally is hard work, skills, and saving.

We all know our children DON'T owe us anything, but in most cases, they couldn't afford to pay us back anyway.

Competing with Technology

- Artificial intelligence will mean computers will do many jobs.

- Customer and processing work, as well as middle management, will disappear.

- Workspaces with rows of desks will no longer exist.

- Almost 50 percent of occupations existing today could be completely redundant by 2025 as artificial intelligence continues to transform businesses.[68]

The good news is the highly skilled will always have more opportunities. The individuals most often affected are those who didn't upgrade their skills or didn't stay relevant in their chosen field.

Social Media and Television

These two activities alone could cost you your retirement. No longer are you keeping up with the Jones but the Kardashians. Based on figures from 2014, the average person watches about 141 hours of TV per month or 1,692 hours per year.[69] Assuming you reach the average U.S. life expectancy of 78, that's about 15 years of your life you're going to spend watching TV. Add five years if you are on social media. Wow! Fifteen to twenty years on entertainment.

I'm suggesting that you either eliminate or limit these two activities. Let's just say you earn $55,000 per year and you cut out these activities and replace them with professional development, health, positive self-talk, or creative pursuits. Here's an example showing the real cost of an overabundant use of social media and television:

Example above $55,000 x 15 =$825,000 or $1,100,000 WOW!!!!

Find out what your number is:

Ranges from _____ Salary x 15 = or
_____ Salary x 20 *both social media and television

Chapter 14

New Age Retirement

"Retirement is not in my vocabulary. They aren't going to get rid of me that way."
— Betty White

Retirement will look very different for each person, but since we are attempting to give you a glimpse of the most common scenarios, these examples of strategies and rules of thumb should give you a guide to what you can expect.

The landscape of retirement has evolved and will continue to evolve as artificial intelligence becomes more relevant. I wanted to highlight the most common sources of income throughout retirement based on your age.

- Millennials and X/Y: No Pension, No Social Security*, Multiple Employers, 401k
- Boomers: Pension, Social Security, Single or Less than three Employers, 401k

If we look at retirement savings as a table with the legs representing different sources of savings, we can visualize retirement funding scenarios. The objective of this chapter is to reshape your expectations and beliefs on what was once called retirement.

Anyone after the Boomers and a significant percentage of Boomers themselves will never fully retire. Many will continue to work longer because of longevity, and others will do so because of need due to lack of planning or lifestyle standards. For the individuals under 45, the retirement landscape has changed forever. Over the next 25-45 years, we are going to experience a wave of older citizens and children of those citizens waiting for them to die so they can live in some cases. How could that possibly happen?

In financial planning, you want everyone to at least have a 401(k), pension, and Social Security, but ideally a plan would include some of the new age retirement income sources like real estate, consulting business, alternative investment, etc.

Median Pension Benefit

In 2015, one out of three older adults received income from a private company or union pension plan, federal, state, or local government pension plan, or Railroad Retirement, military or veterans pension. The median private pension benefit of individuals, aged 65 and older, was $9,376 a year. The median state or local government pension benefit was $16,742.[70]

Median benefit for persons aged 65 and older with income from private pensions and annuities, public pensions, and veterans benefits	
Type of pension benefit	Median benefit, 2015
Private pensions and annuities	$9,376
Federal government pension	$22,669
State or local government pension	$16,742
Railroad pension	$21,017
Military pension	$19,306
Veterans benefits	$11,786

Median Income by Retirement Benefit Type

In 2014, the median income of retiree-aged units (with no earnings from work) aged 65 and over with pensions and Social Security was more than twice the income of aged units receiving only Social Security. [71]

Median annual income of retiree (persons with no earnings) aged units 65 and older, by retirement benefit types	
Retirement benefit type	Median income, 2014
Social Security only	$15,871
Social Security and private pension	$36,270
Social Security and a federal pension	$38,806
Social Security and Railroad Retirement, state, local government or military pension	$37,789

What is the Average (Mean) Retirement Income 2017 What is the Median Retirement Income 2017?

As you can see from the table below, median income is always lower and is probably closer to the reality for most households of retirement age.

The chart below shows the average (mean) retirement income in 2017, which varies significantly by the age of the head of household. Household incomes decline the older they become.[72]

AGE OF HOUSEHOLD	MEDIAN INCOME	MEAN INCOME
Households Aged 55-64	$62,802	$89,986
Households Aged 65-74	$47,432	$68,905
Households Aged 75 and Older	$30,635	$45,989

SOURCE: Data is summarized from the US Census Bureau's Current Population Survey (CPS) Annual Social and Economic (ASEC) Supplement. The CPS is a joint effort between the Bureau of Labor Statistics and the Census Bureau.

Where Does Most Retirement Income Come From?

According to the Pension Rights Center, older adults get retirement income from the following sources:[73]

- Social Security: 85% of people 65 and older get Social Security. The average Social Security income in 2017 is $1,360, according to a fact sheet from the Social Security Administration.

- Assets: 63% of retirees rely on assets for retirement income. According to Retirement USA, "the median amount of asset income for households where either the householder or spouse was aged 65 or older was $1,542 for those households who received any asset income. In 2008, 59% of older households had income from assets."

- Pensions: A mere 32% of today's retirees have pensions, and this number is trending further downward.

- Earnings: 23% of older Americans have work income. According to the AARP, the median retirement income earned by retirees from work is $25,000 a year. Note: This is the largest amount of any income source.

- Public Assistance or Veteran's Benefits: About 7% of retirees are getting help from government sources.[74]

As you can see, retirees today are more dependent than ever before on Social Security income. One of the biggest problems with this approach, aside from the fact that the program isn't incredibly stable, is that Social Security was never intended to be a primary source of income. It was always intended as a boost

For Millennials and X/Y

Stop the search for the magic bullet, shortcut, or perfection. Life has many challenges and rewards that will be reflected in your experiences and choices. These experience and choices will foreshadow your future. The sooner you can identify who you are and not who your parents or the world want you to be; the sooner you can begin the journey of actually living. This will impact your personal and financial goals. Many times you may feel that life is too difficult or you simply don't know where to get started. While at the moment this may be true, if you trust yourself, you will find your way.

Now the money thing and how you have it all. Well, unfortunately only a few can have it all at the same time. Take baby steps about getting started on Project Xero, your skill inventory, and the strategies outlined in this book. Life is a marathon, not a sprint. You won't understand that until later in life when sprinting isn't an option. (Read Chapter 11, Casino Capitalism and Chapter 6, Investment Strategies by Age and Stage)

Boomers and the Well Resourced

Leverage will be the theme of the years to come. You must leverage your relationships, skills, wisdom, and time to maximize this stage of life. Leverage your assets and make sure that you are strategic in everything you do. Les Brown said " On your deathbed how many of your dreams will be standing around you asking you why didn't bring me" As you think about that last question you should also make sure to leverage those dreams by sharing them with the world. How do you take the last 40 years of experience and monetize it in a way that will both keep you relevant *and* enlarge your income and influence? I think you start by reading Skill Monetization. In this chapter, you take a deep look into what you bring to the table and how you can now recreate or re-brand yourself. These are the years where you are the most productive in your field or have the flexibility to change into an entirely different area. Leveraging will be paramount as your work toward staying relevant.

As a financial adviser to retirees, I always hope my clients, at the very least, have retirement savings in a 401(k) or pension. This gives retirees two legs to their retirement table. If they are eligible for Social Security benefits, the table becomes somewhat more stable with three legs; Ideally, however, the table would have a fourth leg by including new age retirement income sources such as real estate or a consulting business. For more ideas on using skills to bring in more income. (Read Chapter 22, Skill Monetization)

Chapter 15

Sudden Wealth

*" Sudden success in golf is like the sudden acquisition of wealth.
It is apt to unsettle and deteriorate the character."*
— P. G. Wodehouse

Sudden wealth seldom happens suddenly, for, as they say, it takes 20 years to become an overnight success. This is because it takes about 20 years to create critical mass or awareness in most fields. See some quick examples below:

What year was television invented? The answer is 1926, but when did most homes get a TV? Early 1950's. The first version of the Internet was created in 1969, but only adopted in the 1990's. There is simply no such thing as sudden wealth.

For example, Mark Rank, professor at Washington University and his co-author Thomas Hirschl of Cornell University followed a group of American adults ages 25-60 over a 44-year period to see what percentage of them reached various levels of income distribution during their lives.

According to Rank, "it turns out that 12% of the population will find themselves in the top 1% of the income distribution for at least one year. What's more, 39% of Americans will spend a year in the top 5% of the income distribution, 56% will find themselves in the top 10%, and a whopping 73% will spend a year in the top 20% of the income distribution."[75]

While many Americans will experience some level of affluence during their lives, a much smaller percentage of them will do so for an extended period. Although 12% of the population will experience a year in which they find themselves in the top 1% of the income distribution, a mere 0.6% will do so in 10 consecutive years."[76]

One of the reasons for such fluidity at the top is that over sufficiently long periods of time, most American households go through a full range of financial experiences, both positive and negative. Rank and Hirschl interviewed individuals who "spoke about hitting a particularly prosperous period where they received a bonus, or a spouse entered the labor market, or there was a change of jobs." These are the types of events that can throw households above particular income thresholds.

As the report notes, "It is clear that the image of a static 1% and 99% is mostly incorrect. The majority of Americans will experience at least one year of affluence at some point during their working careers. (This is just as true at the bottom of the income distribution scale, where 54% of Americans will experience poverty or near poverty at least once between the ages of 25 and 60)".[77]

Ultimately, this information suggests that the United States is indeed a land of opportunity, that the American dream is still possible, but that it is also a land of widespread poverty. And rather than being a place of static, income-based social tiers, America is a place where a vast majority of people will experience either wealth, poverty – or both – during their lifetimes.

Rather than talking about the 1% and the 99% as if they were forever fixed, it would make much more sense to say that Americans are likely to be exposed to both prosperity and poverty during their lives, and to shape our policies accordingly. As such, we have much more in common with one another than we dare to realize.

AFFLUENCE	YEARS	PERCENTAGE
Top 1%	Ten consecutive years	12%
Top 5%	One year or more	39%
Top 10%	One year or more	56%
Top 20%	One year or more	73%

Below is a list that shows that it's not where you are born, but what you do after that makes the difference.

The 20 countries with the most billionaires:

United States	540
China	251
Germany	120
India	84
Russia	77
Hong Kong	64
United Kingdom	50
Italy	43
France	39

Canada	33
Switzerland	32
Brazil	31
South Korea	31
Turkey	30
Japan	27
Sweden	26
Australia	25
Taiwan	25
Spain	21
Indonesia	20

Sudden wealth is only created in three ways:

1. Having a unique intellectual ability or talent, i.e., inventor, surgeon, lawyer, sports, or entertainment (High Earners)

2. Business, real estate, or stock options, i.e., starting a business and selling for a large profit, real estate development or accumulation of property – either residential or commercial (Major investment and risk of time and capital.)

3. Saving and investing over a lifetime. i.e., cash, investment, stock, rental property, and personal property. (This is the most costly, but most standard method, which usually includes many years of hard work).

Income from sudden wealth is more about how much you save than the money you receive. In fact, about 70% of people who win a lottery or get a big windfall end up broke in a few years, according to the National Endowment for Financial Education.[78] We want to share with you the pitfalls and steps to make sure if you have a sudden wealth event you will be adequately prepared.

Just because you come into a large sum of money you shouldn't forget that you are the same person you were before your good fortune. If you are good with money, you will just get better, and if the opposite is true, you will shortly be back to where you started, or worse.

The most difficult part of this process is managing the expectations of friends and family. If you have to support all of your friends and relatives, and they have no way of paying you back if you find yourself in need down the road, it will be taxing both emotionally and financially. You have to have safeguards and systems in place for sudden wealth.

We will talk about the most common scenarios:

These events require you to become the general manager of your life. You will need to hire a business manager, financial planning "team," accountant, business attorney, and estate attorney. After the challenge of creating this team of players, the next hurdle will be controlling friends and family expectations about YOUR money. This can be very challenging. I suggest that you don't do anything in the first six months to a year. This will allows adequate time for you to regain your equilibrium.

The desire to reward yourself and those closest to you is natural, but should not be done without proper planning. The process of setting expectations and realistic goals will help you avoid many of the common pitfalls:

- Not putting enough funds away for taxes on your windfall.

- Purchasing homes without considering maintenance and carrying costs.

- Making investments that have a low probability to contribute to your wealth, such as restaurants, clubs, or exotic investments with the promises of unrealistic returns.

With the proper team around you, these types of opportunities will never be presented to you as they will be evaluated on your behalf and 95% will be rejected before you have to address them. Selling a business, winning the lottery, or joining the right start-up has many benefits, but also several drawbacks if you aren't prepared.

It's important to be aware that in some cases, sudden wealth can bring on depression, disruptive behavior, anxiety attacks, and many other health concerns. These symptoms are so common after a windfall there's even a name for it: Sudden Wealth Syndrome.[79] So don't be alarmed after the dust has settled to notice you have a lot more to the think about, and that those concerns include much larger issues than money.

Six keys to not losing it all:

- Educate yourself on the things that you think you want to invest in before you invest.

- Keep things in perspective and put family first.

- Cash flow and safety should have most of your attention.

- Invest in things you love, and that will appreciate over time.

- Allow the professionals to do their jobs, but don't let them run the show.

- Trust yourself, but verify.

Chapter 16

Escaping the Middle Class

We know what happens to people who stay in the middle of the road. They get run over."
— Ambrose Gwinnett Bierce (1842[1]–circa 1914)
American Civil War soldier, wit, and writer

Although we have progressed in some ways in knocking down stereo-
types as a society, we all face times when those who judge us based
on age, gender, or where we came from still creates impenetrable
walls to clear. Scientist continue to debate whether biases and prejudices are innate or learned, but in either case, 'isms" –ageism, classism,
racism – are alive and well. This doesn't mean there aren't ways to
combat these prejudices. The key is to be consciously aware of the
biases and not to allow them to affect your life or decisions.

This chapter will discuss classism, specifically concerning the
Middle Class. The idea of the middle class is no longer what it once
was. After World War II, the middle class was equated with the
American Dream of upward mobility.[80] Today, it's a place where
Americans get stuck. In a Washington Post article, Lawrence F,
Harvard economist and mobility scholar, explains why moving from
the middle to the upper class has become more difficult in recent
years: "There's so much inequality, people born near the bottom

241

tend to stay near the bottom, and that's much more consequential than it was 50 years ago.[81] In other words, as the wealthy get wealthier, the middle finds it harder to make the jump into the realm of the rich.

For today's middle class, inflation and the cost of living are going up as wages stay the same or decline. Meanwhile, lifestyle expectations are increasing. Retirement was designed based on the middle class. That is why some say retirement no longer exists, that a struggling middle class is not adequately prepared for what was once called retirement.

Staying relevant requires discipline and focus, and an understanding that where you are in the demographic of class structure isn't only about how much a person gets paid. Upper, middle, and lower classes each have distinct ways in which they navigate and communicate within their niche. As Thomas Sowell, a well-respected economist from Stanford has noted, "Wealth begins with culture."[82] The culture and what is important or valued within each of the classes determines your economics.

Being part of the middle class includes inculcating subtle (or sometimes not so subtle) ways of seeing the world. According to a leading U.S. expert on the mindsets of the poor, middle class, and wealthy, Ruby K., Ph.D., the rich simply think differently than the middle class and poor. In her book, *A Framework for Understanding Poverty*, she writes, "each class depends on hidden rules to navigate their social and financial world."[83] Payne asserts that to move up the economic ladder, the rules must be learned and put into practice. For instance, while the driving force for those in poverty is survival, relationships, and entertainment, the middle class is most concerned with work and achievement, and the wealthy are seeking financial, political, and social connections.[84]

Escaping the Middle Class requires planning, commitment, and doing things differently. To make a move, get ready to be comfortable with being uncomfortable. As stated before, the wealthy see the world differently. To escape the Middle Class, you have to learn the different values and worldviews of the wealthy. I recommend purchasing Ruby Payne's book, which outlines these differences. The truth is the middle isn't that bad; it's just not as good as it used to be.

Steps to Escaping the Middle Class

- Start with Project Xero.

- Set goals for the future and write those goals down.

- Share goals with a partner.

- Learn as much as you can about the worldview of the wealthy.

- Work on changing your mindset one step at a time.

Tools and Worksheets:
Escaping the Middle Class

Download a full-sized copy of these resources at:

www.holisticplanners.com

HIDDEN RULES AMONG CLASSES

	POVERTY	MIDDLE CLASS	WEALTH
POSSESSIONS	People.	Things.	One-of-a-kind objects, legacies, pedigrees.
MONEY	To be used, spent.	To be managed.	To be conserved, invested.
PERSONALITY	Is for entertainment. Sense of humor is highly valued.	Is for acquisition and stability. Achievement is highly valued.	Is for connections. Financial, political, social connections are highly valued.
SOCIAL EMPHASIS	Social inclusion of people he/she likes.	Emphasis is on self-governance and self-sufficiency.	Emphasis is on social exclusion.
FOOD	Key question: Did you have enough? Quantity important.	Key question: Did you like it? Quality Important.	Key question: Was it presented well? Presentation important.
CLOTHING	Clothing valued for individual style and expression of personality.	Clothing valued for its quality and acceptance into norm of middle class. Label important.	Clothing valued for its artistic sense and expression. Designer important.

TIME	Present most important. Decisions made for moment based on feelings or survival.	Future most important. Decisions made against future ramifications;	Traditions and history, most important. Decisions mode partially on basis of tradition and decorum.
EDUCATION	Valued and revered as abstract but not as reality.	Crucial for climbing success ladder and making money.	Necessary tradition for making and maintaining connections.
DESTINY	Believes in fate. Cannot do much to mitigate chance.	Believes in choice. Can change future with good choices now.	Noblesse oblige.
LANGUAGE	Casual register. Language is about survival.	Formal register. Language is about negotiation.	Formal register. Language is about networking.
FAMILY STRUCTURE	Tends to be matriarchal.	Tends to be patriarchal.	Depends on who has money.
WORLD VIEW	Sees world in terms of local setting	Sees world in terms of notional setting.	Sees world in terms of international view.
LOVE	Love and acceptance conditional based upon whether	Love and acceptance conditional and based largely upon	Love and acceptance conditional and related to social standing and

	individual is liked.	achievement.	connections.
DRIVING FORCES	Survival, relationships, entertainment.	Work, achievement.	Financial, political, social connections.
HUMOR	About people and sex.	About situations.	About social faux pas.

SOURCE: *Ruby Payne, A Framework for Understanding Poverty. Highlands, TX: aha! Process, Inc., 1996, pp. 42 – 43*

Chapter 17:

Cost of Aging Gracefully and Longevity

"Anyone who stops learning is old, whether at twenty or eighty. Anyone who keeps learning stays young. The greatest thing in life is to keep your mind young."
— Henry Ford

In 1946 the newly founded Gerontological Society of America cited, in the first article of the first issue of its Journal of Gerontology, the need to add "not more years to life, but more life to years."[85]

The goal of staying relevant as you age is a key factor in how healthy and long you live. Is 90 the new 60? No, but with technology and medical breakthroughs, it's much more appealing. Aging can be challenging on many fronts for both men and women, but aging gracefully as you stay relevant is something we all can do.

Exercise Extends Life

You might not be up to pushing the envelope like some of the retirees below, but as stated in Chapter 21, Health: The New Wealth, exercise has multiple longevity benefits.

Let's see a quick example. Meet Ernestine Shepherd. With her flat stomach, toned arms, and excellent health, you'd never guess that this female bodybuilder is in her late 70s. But she is—79, to be exact. As impressive as her physique, one of the most incredible parts of Shepherd's story is that she didn't even start working out until she was 56. This shows that it's never too late for a new beginning.[86]

Another example is 85 year-old Ed Whitlock who is still running marathons. Whitlock's first marathon came in 1975, at age 44, out of parental concern. His youngest son, Clive, 14 at the time, had run every day for a year and wanted to attempt a marathon. "We did our best to try to persuade him out of that," Whitlock said. "He was not to be denied."

Father and son ran in 3:09, and four years later, at 48, Whitlock ran his fastest marathon, in 2:31. He became more devoted to the event after retiring and attempted to become the first person 70 or older to run 26 miles 385 yards in under three hours. In running and exercise science circles, he has become "a rock star,"[87]

As you can see 90 isn't the new 60, but it looks more like it every day.

Obviously, there are costs associated with aging gracefully and living longer, but benefits can't be denied. Political theorist and futurist Francis Fukuyama was particularly eloquent, but hardly alone when he warned two decades ago that if we maintain our obsession with extending life at all costs, society may "increasingly come to resemble a giant nursing home."[88]

The Social Connection

When I was about to graduate from elementary school to middle school, I was excited and looking forward to new experiences. I assumed I would see my old friends daily (or at least Monday through Friday), just as I had always done since kindergarten.

The first day of middle school arrived. I was confused from the moment I stepped through the double doors. In my clenched fist, I held a list of classes I was signed up for, each in a different classroom! Navigation has never been my strong suit and, so needless to say, I was lost most of the day. I had brief glimpses of my friends scurrying through packed hallways to their classes as I frantically looked for classroom numbers.

After a few months, I was able to easily navigate to my classes (except for gym, which was on the other side of the planet from my biology class). One thing did not change at least for the first year of middle school. I no longer saw my friends—friends who I had seen most days of my young life. We had studied together, worked on projects together, had lunch together and most Saturdays "hung out" together. Now, we were in different classes, different activities, and hidden from one another by strangers in crowded hallways. I never felt so alone with so many people around.

The analogy of graduating from elementary school to middle school can explain some of the feelings retirees unexpectedly come up against when "graduating" from work to retirement. While a Merrill Lynch study found that most retirees worry about money, once retired these same people find "their greatest loss [were] their social connections.[89]

Think about it. You've been going to an office, working alongside colleagues, possibly for years. Even with company politics, a majority of the people you worked with were important to you. Colleagues frequently became social friends as well, even if just by having lunch together during the workday. With retirement, the pool of people you communicate with on a daily basis is likely to shrink. This can cause a feeling of isolation.

Lack of social connections is not only bad for your outlook on life, but recent studies have shown that your body and brain also suffer. People who are not lonely tend to be healthier than those who feel isolated. Studies have found that a lack of social connections is just as bad for your health as "smoking 15 cigarettes a day, being an alcoholic or never exercising."[90] Studies also found that retirees with active social connections are less likely to develop dementia.[91] All good news for retirees: seeing friends, family, and participating in life is not only fun but is healthy, too.

It seems the Boomers are having less of a hard time adjusting to life without "work" than one might think. The Merrill Lynch, Age Wave study, found retirees, after a de-stressing phase when they first retire, appear to be making social connections an important part of their lives.[92] Possibly the Boomer generation who are retiring now has gone back to their 1960s philosophy of "chill out." It seems today's retirees just want to have fun and they are looking for experiences as opposed to things.[93]

If you, however, are struggling with the transition, here are some tips:

- Be aware retirement is a transition. Just like other transitions you've experienced in your life, give yourself a break if you're not a social butterfly the moment you stop working.

- Try to maintain friends with your work pals. Meet for lunch. See a movie. If transportation is an issue, think about using the new car services such as Uber and Lyft.

- Get involved with an organization with a mission that means something to you.

- Don't forget social media. Although not as fulfilling as seeing someone in person, linking through social media and video phone calls can help maintain connections you enjoy and care about.

- Think about the "peak" experiences in your life. What made you the happiest? Was it a travel adventure? Check out the resources under 60-70 for travel companies geared to an older clientele.

- Think about those physical activities you like to do? Join a club of like-minded people. Check out the resources under 60-70 for information about biking. If you're looking for less activity, find a book club. The Internet is a good way to find clubs that are in your neighborhood.

- Consider part-time or freelance work in a field of your preference.

Remember, you are an individual, and you may not want to be a "social butterfly." Your retirement is all yours to do with what you will. Embrace who you are and find what will make you happy.

Ultimately, being happy will keep you healthier and add to your longevity.

Chapter 18:

Long-Term Care

"Take care of your body. It's the only place you have to live."
— Jim Rohn

Long-term care is the elephant in the room. Although it's difficult to even think about a time when you might become incapacitated, the statistics are not on your side. Almost 70% of people turning age 65 will need long-term care at some point in their lives.

Researchers James R. Knickman, Ph.D., and Emily Snell, B.A, set out to discover the challenges the Baby Boomer generation will face as they grow older. The results were reported in the *2030 Problem: Caring for Aging Baby Boomers* study.[94]

The researchers found that "as Boomers grow older they will need to prepare for four key financial 'aging shocks': uncovered costs of prescription drugs, costs of medical care not paid by Medicare or private insurance, the actual costs of private insurance that partially fills in the gaps left by Medicare, and uncovered costs of long-term care." Of these four, the study found that "if the lifetime costs of each of these 'aging shocks' are calculated; the long-term care burden is the worst by far."[95]

What is long-term care?

Many of us worry about who would take care of us if something happens. No one wants to be a burden. Long-term care (LTC) is the assistance or supervision you may need when you are not able to do some of the basic activities of daily living (ADL) such as:

- Bathing
- Dressing
- Eating
- Continence
- Toileting
- Moving in and out of bed

The need for long-term care may result from:

- Accident
- Illness
- Advanced aging
- Stroke
- Other chronic condition

Medicare programs do not pay for long-term care. If you or someone you love needs constant care in a facility, your savings could be wiped out within a few years. According to a survey performed by Carescout and posted on the Genworth website, in 2017 the yearly cost of using the services of an adult day care facility would be as much as $18,210. If you need to move to assisted living, the figure goes up to $44,945. A nursing home could cost $95,149 per year. These figures are only a ballpark and will vary according to where you live. Check out Carescout's interactive map for the costs in your state.[96]

If you did drain your savings while living in a long-term care facility, you could at that point claim poverty and apply for services through the Medicaid system. Medicaid does pay for some extended care, but there are restrictions.[97]

This is where long-term care insurance comes in. This type of insurance is a fairly new kid on the block and has been through some growing pains. The recent bad press brought to light that premiums for long-term care insurance have been skyrocketing to such an extent that policyholders who bought the insurance in their 30s or 40s, as was thought prudent, found they could no longer afford the premiums.

Some companies allowed policyholders to freeze their long-term care insurance at the point they could no longer afford the premiums. Although they didn't lose the money they had put in, this arrangement left people without enough money for long-term care. Now the thinking is that long-term care should be purchased around the age of 60, when most people are still healthy. Signing up later saves all the money that would have gone to escalating premiums, making some of that money available for retirement savings.

Basic Long-Term Care Categories

Home care: Ranges from running errands, housekeeping, meal preparation, personal hygiene assistance, to some medical treatment. Home care is designed to help people stay in their homes longer than they otherwise might be able.

Adult day care center: Includes providing social, therapeutic, and health activities in a group setting for people with physical and cognitive needs. An adult day care center typically works best for patients who can sleep through the night in their own home.

Independent-living apartments: Age-restricted communities that traditionally offered no services. In recent years, many of these facilities have added nonmedical services such as transportation, dining, and concierge desks. These services can be combined with home-health care if needed.

Assisted-living facilities: These facilities provide help with daily-living activities, but not necessarily 24-hour skilled-nursing care. Experts recommend trying to pay for services that are needed a la carte rather than paying for bundled packages.

Skilled-nursing facilities: Commonly called nursing homes, these facilities offer the most comprehensive level of care and typically are the most expensive option.

Continuing-care retirement communities: These facilities typically offer progressive care, starting with apartments or houses where older adults can live independently. As more services are needed, residents move to different parts of the community where physicians and medical treatments are easily available. The drawback: These facilities typically require large lump sum payments upon entry, and sometimes also steep monthly fees.

Hospice care: Intended for patients in the last stages of a terminal illness, hospice focuses on palliative care, providing relief from symptoms, pain, and stress, and making patients comfortable. Medicare sometimes covers hospice.

Share-Care

If you are a couple thinking about long-term care, the cost for two policies can be prohibitive. A share-care policy allows couples to purchase one policy, with each person becoming a rider on the policy. This allows the couple to share the benefits. The benefits of share-care are that it's cheaper than buying two policies while mitigating the risk that someone you love will end up in poverty.

For example, if Bill and Margaret bought a 6-year share-care policy, they would be able to share the benefits at a much cheaper cost than if they bought two 6-year policies. If Bill eventually needs long-term care, the policy pays for the cost. Without the policy, Margaret would need to tap into savings to pay for Bill's care, potentially leaving her destitute. If Bill dies two years after being in long-term care, Margaret can tap into the remainder of the 4 years in benefits when needed.[98]

LGBT Long-Term Care

Among LGBT elders, many singles and couples are estranged from their families of birth. Many in the LGBT community are reliant on "families of choice" for their support. As defined by the National Resource Center on LGBT Aging, these are diverse family structures that:

- Are usually created by LGBT people, immigrants, and racial or ethnic minorities.
- Include but are not limited to, life partners, close friends, and other loved ones not biologically related or legally recognized.

- Are the source of social and caregiving support.
- Provided a tremendous amount of support to gay men during the early years of the AIDS epidemic.
- Tend to be from the same age cohort. For the aging LGBT population, this may mean that many in their families of choice are also in need of support and services at the same time. Therefore, they may not be available to provide the level of support needed.

A major question often faced by those needing long-term care is, "Do I have family members who will provide care?" Whether you have a family of choice, family of origin, or both to assist you in the event you need long-term support and services, plan with your 'family' now and begin to talk with your loved ones to develop a plan of care.[99]

Shopping for Long-Term Care

Before purchasing a policy, consumers should make sure they understand exactly what's covered and what isn't. Avoid purchasing policies from insurers who do not have a solid financial background, and check into how many complaints have been filed against them for non-payment of services. All insurance companies are rated by agencies such as A.M Best, Standard & Poor's, and Moody's.[100]

Tools and Worksheets:
Long-Term Care

Download a full-sized copy of these resources at:

www.holisticplanners.com

Long-term care planning

LONG-TERM VISION

Many individuals will need long-term care, which often starts with home care and progresses to a nursing home.

- There is a 1 in 3 chance that a long-term care need will last less than 6 months, but there is a 1 in 10 chance it will last 5 or more years.

Likelihood of needing long-term care LT

Spending

■ Men ■ Women

1 new LT claims by type

Average age of first claim: 9

51.0%
30.5%
18.5%

All LT claims by type

58.0%
25.0%
17.0%

■ Home care ■ Assisted living ■ Nursing home

Source: American Association for Long-Term Care Insurance 2014 Sourcebook, www.aaltci.org. Annualized inflation 1994-2012: 3.81% nursing home care; 1.67% home health care.

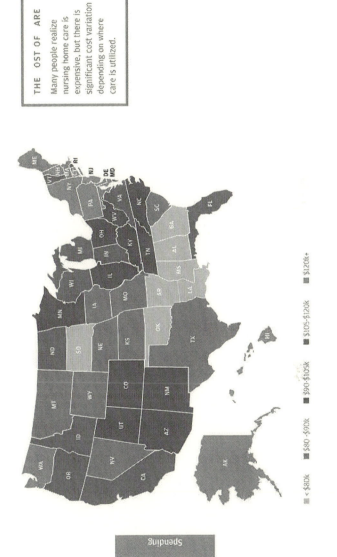

Annual cost of nursing home care (private room)

THE OST OF ARE

Many people realize nursing home care is expensive, but there is significant cost variation depending on where care is utilized.

Spending

■ < $80k   ■ $80-$90k   ■ $90-$105k   ■ $105-$120k   ■ $120k+

Source: New York Life Insurance 2014 Cost of Care Survey developed in partnership with Univita. Average daily costs annualized over 365 days and weighted by city population for each state.

GERIATRIC DEPRESSION SCALE(GDS)

The Geriatric Depression Scale (GDS) is a simple, 30-item, yes/no questionnaire that can be helpful in identifying possible depression among elderly people.

Please answer "yes" or "no" to the following questions in regards to how you have been feeling recently.

RADICAL HONESTY	CIRCLE ONE
1. Are you basically satisfied with your life?	Yes or No
2. Have you dropped many of your activities and interests?	Yes or No
3. Do you feel that your life is empty?	Yes or No
4. Do you often get bored?	Yes or No
5. Are you hopeful about the future?	Yes or No
6. Are you bothered by thoughts you can't get out of your head?	Yes or No
7. Are you in good spirits most of the time?	Yes or No
8. Are you afraid that something bad is going to happen to you?	Yes or No
9. Do you feel happy most of the time?	Yes or No
10. Do you often feel helpless?	Yes or No
11. Do you often get restless and fidgety?	Yes or No
12. Do you prefer to stay at home, rather than going out and doing new things?	Yes or No

13. Do you frequently worry about the future?	Yes or No
14. Do you feel you have more problems with memory than most?	Yes or No
15. Do you think it is wonderful to be alive now?	Yes or No
16. Do you often feel downhearted and blue?	Yes or No
17. Do you feel pretty worthless the way you are now?	Yes or No
18. Do you worry a lot about the past?	Yes or No
19. Do you find life very exciting?	Yes or No
20. Is it hard for you to get started on new projects?	Yes or No
21. Do you feel full of energy?	Yes or No
22. Do you feel that your situation is hopeless?	Yes or No
23. Do you think that most people are better off than you are?	Yes or No
24. Do you frequently get upset over little things?	Yes or No
25. Do you frequently feel like crying?	Yes or No
26. Do you have trouble concentrating?	Yes or No
27. Do you enjoy getting up in the morning?	Yes or No
28. Do you prefer to avoid social gatherings?	Yes or No
29. Is it easy for you to make decisions?	Yes or No
30. Is your mind as clear as it used to be?	Yes or No

Background

The Geriatric Depression Scale (GDS) is a 30-item self-report assessment used to identify depression in the elderly. The scale was first developed in 1982 by J.A. Yesavage and others.[1]

The scale consists of 30 yes/no questions. Each question is scored as either 0 or 1 points. The following general cutoff may be used to qualify the severity: **A diagnosis of clinical depression should not be based on GDS results alone.**

- Normal 0-9,
- Mild depressed 10-19
- Very depressed 20-30.

Disclaimer

We are not medical or psychiatric professionals. The information provided in this book is for educational and entertainment purposes only. The assessments in this book are not intended to diagnose any disease or condition and should not be solely relied on, even by mental health or health care professionals, for this or any similar purpose.

No one other than a trained mental health professional can diagnose or treat a psychological condition. If you have any concerns about your health, please talk to a professional.

Sources

1.JA Yesavage, TL Brink, et al. Development and Validation of a Geriatric Depression Screening Scale: a Preliminary Report. 17(1): J Psychiatr Res. 37-49. 1983.
2.JI Sheikh, JA Yesavage. Geriatric Depression Scale (GDS): Recent Evidence and Development of a Shorter Version. 5(1/2): Clin Gerontol 165-173. 1986.

3.EL Lesher, JS Berryhill. Validation of the Geriatric Depression Scale-Short Form Among Inpatients. 50(2): J Clin Psychol 256-260. 1994.

Chapter 19

A-Bomb

"Alzheimer's caregivers are heroes."
— Leeza Gibbons

She called it "the long goodbye," words that will resonate with anyone caring for a loved one with Alzheimer's disease. By the time President Reagan died from complications of Alzheimer's, his wife, Nancy, had taken care of her husband for a decade.

Many diseases are cruel, but Alzheimer's is right up there with the cruelest. It starts innocently enough—a few missed words, retelling a story just told, forgetting what was once easy to remember. Difficulties that can be easily excused with, "I'm just getting old."

Dementia vs. Alzheimer's

Dementia is an overarching term for disease that causes cognitive impairment. Alzheimer's is a type of dementia. Both diseases have some overlap in symptoms, but AD has specific symptoms, which are not seen in other types of dementia.[101]

269

Alzheimer's Defined

Someone is diagnosed with Alzheimer's disease every sixty-six seconds in the United States.[102] Alzheimer's is an irreversible, progressive brain disorder that slowly destroys memory and thinking skills, and eventually the ability to carry out the simplest tasks. In most people with Alzheimer's, symptoms first appear in their mid-60s. Estimates vary, but experts suggest that more than 5 million Americans may have Alzheimer's."[103]

Early signs and symptoms

So how do you know if you're showing signs of Alzheimer's? According to a study conducted by Daniel Marson, neurology professor and director of the Alzheimer's Disease Center at the University of Alabama, Birmingham and reported by Kimberly Blanton in the Squared Away Blog, there are some early warning signs. Surprisingly, one particular lost skill could be the "canary in the coal mine."[104]

That skill? A sudden difficulty in managing financial tasks, such as confusion when paying bills, and arithmetic mistakes or trouble balancing a checkbook. However, these are only signs if the person was able to perform these tasks at one time.[105] Other memory problems are also among the first signs of cognitive impairment related to Alzheimer's disease. For many, decline in non-memory aspects of cognition, such as word-finding, vision/spatial issues, and impaired reasoning or judgment, may signal the very early stages of Alzheimer's disease.[106]

Mild Alzheimer' Disease

As the disease progresses, people experience greater memory loss and other cognitive difficulties. Problems can include:

- Wandering and getting lost

- Trouble handling money and paying bills

- Repeating questions

- Taking longer to complete normal daily tasks

- Losing things or misplacing them in odd places

- Personality and behavior changes

- Alzheimer's disease is often diagnosed at this stage.[107]

Moderate Alzheimer's Disease

In this stage, damage occurs in areas of the brain that control language, reasoning, sensory processing, and conscious thought. These symptoms may include:

- Increased memory loss and confusion

- Problems recognizing family and friends

- Inability to learn new things

- Difficulty carrying out multi-step tasks such as getting dressed

- Problems coping with new situations

- Hallucinations, delusions, and paranoia

- Impulsive behavior[108]

Severe Alzheimer's Disease

People with severe Alzheimer's cannot communicate and are completely dependent on others for their care. Near the end, the person may be in bed most or all of the time as the body shuts down. Their symptoms often include:

- Inability to communicate

- Weight loss

- Seizures

- Skin infections

- Difficulty swallowing

- Groaning, moaning, or grunting

- Increased sleeping

- Lack of bowel and bladder control[109]

Diagnosing

Getting a precise diagnosis can help you get started on planning for the care and support you might need. The earlier you detect Alzheimer's, the better chance you have of treatments possibly delaying certain symptoms. Early diagnosis also allows families to better plan for the course of the disease.

When someone tells a doctor about memory problems, the doctor may check their overall health, review medicines they take, and conduct or order tests that test memory, problem-solving, counting, and language skills. Sometimes, a brain scan (a CT, MRI, or other tests) might help determine whether memory complaints are caused by another condition or Alzheimer's.

If a primary care doctor suspects possible Alzheimer's, he or she may refer you to a specialist who can provide a detailed diagnosis, or you may decide to go to an expert on your own. You can find professionals through memory clinics and centers, or through local organizations or referral services.

Specialists include:

Geriatricians: They manage health care in older adults. They know how the body changes as it ages and whether symptoms indicate a serious problem.

Geriatric psychiatrists: These professionals specialize in the mental and emotional health of older adults and can assess memory and thinking problems.

Neurologists: They specialize in the health of the brain and central nervous system and can conduct and review brain scans (including CTs and MRIs, as well as other tests).

Neuropsychologists: They can conduct tests of memory and thinking.

Memory clinics and centers: These have teams of specialists who work together to diagnose the problem.

Tests: Often performed at the clinic or center, which can speed up diagnosis.

The NIH Alzheimer's Disease Education and Referral Center offers more information on getting a diagnosis, as well as the latest methods for diagnosis. The NIH also provides a list of research facilities across the country.

The Mayo Clinic's Alzheimer resources provide an overview of various tests doctors may perform in their office or order to be done in a separate appointment. The Alzheimer's Association has information on finding a physician, and the steps physicians will take during the medical evaluation.[110]

Tools and Worksheets:
A-Bomb

Alzheimer's Disease Statistics	Data
Number of Americans who are living with Alzheimer's disease	5,000,000
Percent of assisted living residents with Alzheimer's disease and other dementias	41.8%
Number of nursing home residents with Alzheimer's	231,900
Percent of nursing home residents with Alzheimer's	15.5%
Percent of seniors who die with Alzheimer's or some form of dementia	33%
Number of deaths each year due to Alzheimer's	84,974
Cause of death rank	6th
Percent of Alzheimer's patients who are women	66%
Annual cost of Alzheimer's patient care in the U.S.	$220,000,000,000
Every 67 seconds someone in the United States develops Alzheimer's.	
Alzheimer's disease doubles every five years beyond age 65.	

Racial Makeup of Alzheimer's	Percent
Ages 65–74	
White	2.9%
African American	9.1%
Hispanic	7.5%
Ages 75–84	
White	10.9%
African American	19.9%
Hispanic	27.9%
85 Years and Older	
White	30.2%
African American	58.6%
Hispanic	62.9%

Sources: Alzheimer's Association

Chapter 20

Conversations that Matter

"The greatest legacy one can pass on to one's children and grandchildren is not money or other material things accumulated in one's life, but rather a legacy of character and faith."
— Billy Graham

The conversation around your mortality is the most important financial topic of all, but the most often overlooked or avoided.

The reason that it matters so much is that without this conversation, your heirs are left to assume what you would have wanted. In some cases they may be unprepared to handle your affairs in the manner that you would have wished. Starting the conversation early is the ideal situation because it's so far away that it will allow time to revise and modify. Frequently, this conversation is centered on what the wishes of your loved one are after death, but families should also discuss issues such as future disability or the need for long-term care.

The conversation doesn't have to be drawn out or dramatic, but I think it should go beyond the standard legal and financial items – although it is imperative to have those items organized. Family videos, family history, documenting, and recording later generation's core value statement and individual wishes are just a few items we have found that have made a tremendous impact in the lives of our clients. The National Institute on Aging lists the relevant documents that are a must, divided into personal, financial, and legal documents.

Personal Records

- Full legal name

- Social Security number

- Legal residence

- Date and place of birth

- Names and addresses of spouse and children

- Location of birth and death certificates, certificates of marriage, divorce, citizenship, and adoption

- Employers and dates of employment

- Education and military records

- Names and phone numbers of religious contacts

- Memberships in groups and awards received

- Names and phone numbers of close friends, relatives, doctors, lawyers, and financial advisors

- Medications taken regularly (be sure to update this regularly)

- Location of living will and other legal documents[111]

Financial Records

- Sources of income and assets (pension from your employer, IRAs, 401(k)s, interest, etc.)

- Social Security and Medicare/Medicaid information

- Insurance information (life, health, long-term care, home, car) with policy numbers, agents' names and phone numbers

- Names of your banks and account numbers (checking, savings, credit union)

- Investment income (stocks, bonds, property) and stockbrokers' names and phone numbers

- Copy of most recent income tax return

- Location of most up-to-date will with an original signature

- Liabilities, including property tax (what is owed, to whom, and when payments are due)

- Mortgages and debts (how and when they are paid)

- Location of original deed of trust for home

- Car title and registration

- Credit and debit card names and numbers

- Location of safe deposit box and key[112]

Legal Documents

- Wills and trusts let you name the person you want your money and property to go to after you die.

- An advanced directive or living will gives you a say in your health care if you become too ill to make your wishes known. In a living will, you can state what kind of care you do or don't want. This can make it easier for family members to make tough health care decisions for you.

- For legal matters, there are two ways to give someone you trust the power to act in your place:

  o A general power of attorney lets you give someone else the authority to act on your behalf. This power will end if you are unable to make your own decisions.

  o A durable power of attorney allows you to name someone to act on your behalf for any legal task. It stays in place if you become unable to make your own decisions.

- You may want to talk to a lawyer about setting up a general power of attorney, durable power of attorney, joint account, trust, or advance directive. Be sure to ask about the lawyer's fees before you make an appointment.[113]

As you can see, there's a lot of information to gather. Organization is essential if you don't want to drown in paper. The National Institute on Aging has some tips:

- Put your important papers and copies of legal documents in one place. You can set up a file, put everything in a desk or dresser drawer, or list the information and location of papers in a notebook. If your papers are in a bank safe deposit box, keep copies in a file at home. Check each year to see if there's anything new to add.

- Tell a trusted family member or friend where you put all your important papers. You don't need to tell this friend or family member about your personal affairs, but someone should know where you keep your documents in case of an emergency. If you don't have a relative or friend you trust, ask a lawyer to help.

- Give permission in advance for your doctor or lawyer to talk with your caregiver as needed. There may be questions about your care, a bill, or a health insurance claim. Without your consent, your caregiver may not be able to get needed information. You can give your okay in advance to Medicare, a credit card company, your bank, or your doctor. You may need to sign and return a form.[114]

- If you truly want to cut down on paper, create a file on your computer. Many forms may already be digitized. If not, make a scan. Back up all this information on a USB drive so if something goes wrong with your computer, you still have the information.

Estate Planning

Estate Planning can get lost in the mix of the other issues you may be dealing with at this time. It's important to plan for any large transfers of money. If at some point you or a loved one needs to access Medicaid benefits (See Chapter 23 for an explanation of Medicaid), the government will review your asset transfer. If you are not compliant you could be penalized.

Medicaid was created for those who have very few resources, so this rule is an attempt to discourage hiding assets to be eligible for Medicaid. If you do need Medicaid before the end of the look-back period, you will be penalized. The penalty period is based on dividing the amount transferred by the average cost of a nursing home in your state. In 2006, Congress raised the asset transfer look-back period from 3 to 5 years, as part of the Deficit Reduc-tion Act (DRA).

The rule for transferring assets is complicated. The basics will be discussed in the following paragraphs, but I strongly advise you to contact an elder law attorney before beginning the process of dispersing assets.

If you need Medicaid financial help for long-term care before the 5 year look-back period is up, you will be penalized. The penalty is a period when you will be ineligible for Medicaid and is calcu-lated by dividing the amount transferred by what Medicaid deter-mines to be the average cost of a nursing home in your state.[115] The United States is lagging behind other parts of the world when it comes to leaving inheritances for future generations.

Chapter 21

Health: The New Wealth

"It is health that is real wealth and not pieces of gold and silver."
— Mahatma Gandhi

Two things that we can't purchase or replace: time and health.

It stands to reason that we should take the time to manage our health. Today we have more unhealthy adults than ever before living in the United States. The cost of being sick outweighs the discipline of doing a few small things daily to remain healthy. Dr. Michael Greger, M.D. FACLM, founder of the popular website NutritionFacts.org reveals the groundbreaking scientific evidence behind the only diet that can prevent and reverse many of the causes of disease-related death.[116] I would highly recommend you purchase his book. It can help you protect and preserve your wealth, but only you can take the steps Dr. Greger suggests.

Fidelity Benefits Consulting has been tracking retiree health care costs for over a decade. According to their latest study, a 65 year-old couple retiring in 2016 with an average life expectancy of an 85 year-old man and an 87-year-old female will need an average of $260,000 for medical expenses. This figure does not include nursing home care and assumes you are eligible to sign up for Medi-care.[117] A couple may need to spend almost $400,000 on health care in retirement.[118]

So what's a future retiree to do?

Get or stay healthy at whatever age you are now. At the risk of sounding like a fitness and nutrition book, this is a topic rarely mentioned when talking about finances. Getting sick is expensive. Sometimes getting sick can't be avoided—things happen—but there are ways to prevent the ailments that will follow you into re-tirement and drain your account.

If you eat a lot of junk food, it's time to think of that burger loaded with grease, sugar, and starch, as taking money from your retirement. In 2015 the Center for Nutrition Policy and Promo-tion published guides for healthy eating:

Healthy Eating As We Age

As we age, healthy eating can make a difference in our health, help to improve how we feel, and encourage a sense of well-being. Eat-ing healthy has benefits that can help older adults.

Nutrients

- Obtain nutrients such as potassium, calcium, vitamin D, vi-tamin B_{12}, minerals, and dietary fiber that are needed by your body.

- Lose weight or maintain a healthy weight.

- Reduce the risk of developing chronic diseases such as high blood pressure, diabetes, hypertension, and heart disease. If you have a chronic disease, eating well can help you manage the disease.

- Meet individual calorie and nutrition needs.

- Help to maintain energy levels.

Special Nutrition Concerns for Older Adults

Our daily eating habits change as our bodies get older. Make small adjustments to help you enjoy the foods and beverages you eat and drink:

- Add flavor to foods with spices and herbs instead of salt, and look for low-sodium packaged foods.

- Add sliced fruits and vegetable to your meals and snacks. Look for pre-sliced fruits and vegetables on sale if slicing and chopping is a challenge.

- Ask your doctor to suggest other options if the medications you take affect your appetite or change your desire to eat.

- Drink three cups of fat-free or low-fat milk throughout the day. If you cannot tolerate milk, try small amounts of yogurt, buttermilk, hard cheese, or lactose-free foods. Drink water instead of sugary drinks.

- Consume foods fortified with vitamin B12, such as fortified cereals.

- With age, you may lose some of your sense of thirst. Drink water often. Low-fat or fat-free milk or 100% juice also helps you stay hydrated. Limit beverages that have lots of added sugars or salt.[119]

Be Active Your Way

Focus on maintaining a healthy body weight. Being physically active can help you stay strong and independent as you grow older. If you are overweight or obese, weight loss can improve your quality of life and reduce the risk of disease and disability.

- Adults at any age need at least 2 ½ hours, or 150 minutes, of moderate-intensity physical activity each week. Being active at least three days a week is a good goal

- Include activities that improve balance and reduce your risk of falling, such as lifting small weights. Add strength-building activities at least two times per week.

- Being active will make it easier to enjoy other activities such as shopping, playing a sport, or gardening.

- If you are not sure about your level of fitness, check with your doctor before starting an intense exercise program or vigorous physical activity.

The USDA developed the pyramid below to allow a quick understanding of what foods should be eaten and in what proportions.

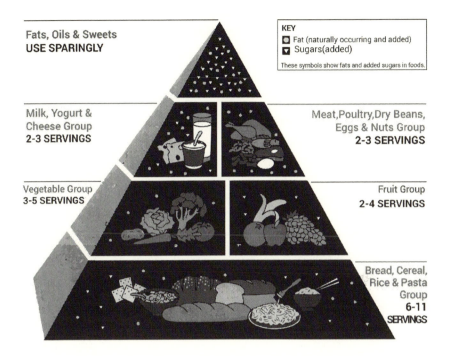

Fats, Oils & Sweets
USE SPARINGLY

KEY
☐ Fat (naturally occurring and added)
▼ Sugars(added)
These symbols show fats and added sugars in foods.

Milk, Yogurt &
Cheese Group
2-3 SERVINGS

Meat,Poultry,Dry Beans,
Eggs & Nuts Group
2-3 SERVINGS

Vegetable Group
3-5 SERVINGS

Fruit Group
2-4 SERVINGS

Bread, Cereal,
Rice & Pasta
Group
6-11
SERVINGS

Exercising

Of course, you probably already know this, but it bears repeating, exercising is critical for your health and should be a part of your everyday routine before retirement and after. We all know that exercise controls weight, reducing the risk of cardiovascular disease, Type 2 Diabetes, and some cancers. The importance of exercise to maintain healthy bones and a sense of balance is sometimes overlooked.

As you grow older bones can be weakened, in men as well as women, but particularly in women, causing curved spinal columns and brittle bones. Combine brittle bones with poor balance, and you're looking at a broken hip just waiting to happen. A broken hip in old age is a tough convalesce and will be expensive.

According to the Centers for Disease Control (CDC), 95% of factures are caused by falls (and falls frequently happen due to lack of balance).[120] One in five patients suffering a broken hip will die within a year of the injury.

Strength and balance exercises can help prevent fractures. Yoga is one good example of an exercise that is good for bones and balance. Lifting weights contributes to keeping bones strong. There are specific balance exercises. Meredith Mickelson, MS, located in the Washington, DC metropolitan area, also recommends the Melt Method®, which works on body alignment, posture, and stability to lessen the risk of falls.[121]

A trainer specializing in elder activities is great, but not always affordable. As minimal equipment is needed, for a small fee, some trainers are happy to set up a home program that you can do yourself. Many free or lowcost options can be found through videos on the internet, books, local programs, and the YMCA. These also require minimal equipment.

Healthy.gov recommends the following:

18-64 years
All adults should avoid inactivity. Some physical activity is better than none, and adults who participate in any amount of physical activity gain some health benefits.

For substantial health benefits, adults should do at least 150 minutes (2 hours and 30 minutes) a week of moderate-intensity, or 75 minutes (1 hour and 15 minutes) a week of vigorous-intensity aerobic physical activity, or an equivalent combination of moderate- and vigorous-intensity aerobic activity. Aerobic activity should be performed in episodes of at least 10 minutes, and preferably, should be spread throughout the week.

For additional and more extensive health benefits, adults should increase their aerobic physical activity to 300 minutes (5 hours) a week of moderate-intensity, or 150 minutes a week of vigorous-intensity aerobic physical activity, or an equivalent combination of moderate- and vigorous-intensity activity. Additional health benefits are gained by engaging in physical activity beyond this amount.

Adults should also include muscle-strengthening activities that involve all major muscle groups on 2 or more days a week.[122]

65 years and older

Older adults should follow the adult guidelines. When older adults cannot meet the adult guidelines, they should be as physically active as their abilities and conditions will allow.

Older adults should do exercises that maintain or improve balance if they are at risk of falling.

Older adults should determine their level of effort for physical activity relative to their level of fitness.

Older adults with chronic conditions should understand whether and how their conditions affect their ability to do regular physical activity safely.

Keeping healthy throughout your life will allow you to live a life worth living.[123]

Healthcare lecture over.

Tools and Worksheets:
Health: The New Wealth

Download a full-sized copy of these resources at:

www.holisticplanners.com

NUMBERS YOU NEED TO KNOW

ITEMS	MEN	WOMEN
1	2,550 Calories per day*if you need to lose weight consume 500 less	2,000*if you need to lose weight consume 500 less
2	For men, risk increases with a measurement when your waist is over 40 inches.	For women, health risk begins to rise when your waist is more than 35 inches.
3	When you see your doctor for blood test results, ask for the readings for both forms of cholesterol and the ratio of your total cholesterol to HDLs (TC:HDL). Aim for total cholesterol below 5.2 mmol/l (below 5 mmol/l if you have heart disease or diabetes), and LDL cholesterol levels below 3.5 mmol/l, or below 2 mmol/l if you have a history of heart disease. A	When you see your doctor for blood test results, ask for the readings for both forms of cholesterol and the ratio of your total cholesterol to HDLs (TC:HDL). Aim for total cholesterol below 5.2 mmol/l (below 5 mmol/l if you have heart disease or diabetes), and LDL

	healthy HDL level is 1.3 mmol/l or above.	cholesterol levels below 3.5 mmol/l, or below 2 mmol/l if you have a history of heart disease. A healthy HDL level is 1.3 mmol/l or above.
4	A reading of 140/90 mm Hg or more is considered high, and if it's between 120/80 and 139/89, you may still be at risk and should be taking steps to prevent the development of hypertension.	A reading of 140/90 mm Hg or more is considered high, and if it's between 120/80 and 139/89, you may still be at risk and should be taking steps to prevent the development of hypertension.
5	A normal resting pulse rate is 60 to 90 beats per minute	For example, a normal resting pulse rate is 60 to 90 beats per minute
6	A normal triglyceride reading is less than 1.7 mmol/l .	A normal triglyceride reading is less than 1.7 mmol/l .It's normal

		to have some triglycerides in your bloodstream, but high levels are linked to coronary artery disease—especially in women.
7	Body Mass Index (BMI) Goal: 18.5 to 24.9	Body Mass Index (BMI) Goal: 18.5 to 24.9

Source: Readers Digest

KEY: Health is Wealth

YOUR NUMBERS		
	CURRENT	GOAL 12-24 MONTHS
CALORIES PER DAY		
WAIST		
HDL LEVELS		
BLOOD PRESSURE		
RESTING HEART RATE		
TRIGLYCERIDE		
BODY MASS INDEX (BMI)		
SHORT TERM MEMORY*BONUS		

100% of your attention should be given to eliminating ANY health concerns

Chapter 22

Skill Monetization

"Mom was 50 when my Dad died. She got on a bus every weekday for years, and rode 40 miles each morning to Madison. She earned a new degree and learned new skills to start her small business. It wasn't just a new livelihood. It was a new life."
— Paul Ryan

Most believe the myth that life is about money or things, but life is all about collecting skills.

Money and things can be easily replaced if you have the proper skills. You will need to break down your skills and talents so that you are better able to know your true value. Understanding your human potential is the quickest way to health, wealth, and happiness. How do you monetize your MBA or Ph.D., a thirty-year career, or a database of relationships that you've built over the years? This should be done very strategically with the end goal in mind. Many people go through life and minimize their value. They don't recognize the enormous value of specialized skills.

As you will see in this chapter, it's never too late to maximize or monetize the knowledge you bring to the table. We've identified traditional approaches that will not work in the new world of retirement. I've also mentioned numerous times throughout this book, that Social Security and savings may not be enough to see you through your retirement. Here's where all that reflection you did during the first part of the book begins to kick in.

You should start thinking of ways to monetize your skills years before retirement, but if you haven't don't panic; just take some time to reflect. Ask yourself, "What skills do I have that I can monetize either in a full-time or part-time job?" "Would I like to try my hand at something entirely new?" "Do I finally want to get that Master's degree to teach?" Look into classes or educational opportunities to gain the skills you need and strategize how to use those skills in a full or part-time job or even as the basis for creating your own company. The best of all worlds is to find something you are passionate about or have wanted to pursue for a long time, but couldn't when you were working. Hopefully, you can schedule within your new work life some flexibility and time for non-work activities.

New technology has given birth to the gig economy. If you have a special or marketable skill, such as handyman, computer programmer, social media aficionado, you can sign up online with a company that can help you find clients. There are even sites like Wyzant that match knowledgeable people in particular subjects or skills with people who want to learn those skills. If you have an extra room or two in your house, Airbnb might be an option, or driving for Uber could help increase your income. Welcome to the new gig economy, which allows you to use your skills and knowledge, but still gives the flexibility you want at this time of life.

Knowing the stories of people who have successfully remained relevant or reinvented themselves at the time when they could have been planted in a rocking chair is an inspiration. These people are no different than you. They just had the motivation and confidence to try something new.

Kentucky Fried Chicken and Col. Sanders (1890-1980)

One of the oldest success stories of someone remaining relevant during what should have been his retirement years is the owner of Kentucky Fried Chicken, Harlan David Sanders, aka Colonel Sanders. At the age of 65, Sanders started frying chicken for a living. In his youth, Sanders worked many different jobs from farming to steamboat pilot, to an insurance salesman. When he turned 40 years old, he started a service station and sold chicken dinners to his patrons. Over some years he developed a way to pressure fry the chicken. As the demand for his special chicken grew, he opened a restaurant. As fate would have it, a major interstate was built, which diverted traffic away from the road his restaurant was on. Sanders decided to franchise his business, and Kentucky Fried Chicken was born.

McDonald's and Ray Kroc

Ray Kroc started McDonald's at age 52, in 1964. At that time, most people his age would be thinking about retiring. Kroc was a milkshake machine salesman. One day he happened on a hamburger stand in San Bernardino, California. Instead of selling the McDonald brothers his machine, he bought their business. The rest is one of the greatest success stories. Ray Kroc became a pioneer in the fast food industry. He started a uniform system of production for hamburgers, milkshakes, and French fries so that the food tasted the same in each of the franchises throughout the country, and eventually the world. In 1960, Kroc had more than 200 McDonald franchises in the United States, but he barely earned a profit. Prosperity began when he started the Franchise Realty Corporation, which bought up property and leased it to franchisees. With the profits from real estate, Kroc started advertising to support the franchises and, in the 1970's, expanded across the globe. From creating assembly line food production to welcoming ideas from his franchisees, McDonald's has known great success and is often a model for other fast food establishments. Kroc went on to accumulate $500 million dollars in assets. [124]

JC Penney and James Cash Penney (1875-1971)

Of course, the best-laid plans don't always go smoothly. Sometimes it takes a little dip in the mountain before you reach the summit. A case in point is the story of JC Penny. The road to fame and fortune didn't always run smoothly for Penney. With the 1929 stock market crash, Penney lost $40 million when several banks from which he had borrowed foreclosed on loans secured by his personal holdings of stock. At the age of 56, he was $7 million in debt. But Penney was able to start over again with borrowed money and soon regained control of his "empire." In his later years, he reflected, "I believe in adherence to the Golden Rule, faith in God and the country. If I were a young man again, those would be my cardinal principles." [125]

If your skills or your passions lean toward more creative areas, here's a list of late-blooming writers and artists to get you inspired.

Penelope Fitzgerald (1916-2000)

Penelope Fitzgerald grew up in an exceptional and eccentric family. Scholars and the clergy hung from just about every branch of the family tree. Her father dabbled in the theater and was also the editor of Punch, a British satirical magazine. Penelope married Desmond Fitzgerald, a lawyer, in 1942, just before Desmond headed off to war. Desmond's war experience involved heavy fighting in Italy. He returned "a different person from the dashing young officer Penelope had married." Desmond became an alcoholic and was eventually disbarred for "forging signatures on checks that he cashed at a pub." By 1953 the family, which at this point included one son and two daughters, was poverty stricken. They moved onto a houseboat that their son, Valpy, called "a total disaster area". With a husband who frequently came home drunk and could only find low-paying jobs, it was up to Penelope to figuratively and literally keep her family afloat. Her attempts weren't always successful. After three years of close quarters, pools of water in the living room at high tide, and beating backwater rats, the boat sank in the Thames. The wreckage was towed away with all their possessions. For the next eight years, the family lived in a homeless shelter and public housing. Desmond died in 1975. In 1977 at the age of 60, Penelope wrote her first novel, The Golden Child. Along with writing three biographies, a collection of short stories, essays, and reviews, she would go on to write 8 more novels: The Bookshop, 1978 (shortlisted Booker Prize); Offshore, 1979 (Booker Prize); Human Voices, 1980; At Freddie's, 1982; Innocence, 1986; The Beginning of Spring, 1988; The Gate of Angels, 1990 (shortlisted Booker Prize), and The Blue Flower, 1990 (The Observer called it one of the ten best historical novels).[126]

Grandma Moses (1860-1961)

Anna Mary Robertson, better known as Grandma Moses, grew up on a farm in Greenwich, New York. Although her family was poor and needed all hands to work the farm, Anna did go to school for a short time. There she was introduced to painting. At the age of 27, she married Thomas Salmon Moses. Five of the ten children born to the couple survived infancy. Thomas and Anna continued to work on a farm. Even with the long hours and hard work, Anna took the time to create a decorative home, painting a fireboard using house paint and embroidering pictures. When she developed arthritis and embroidering became too painful, she turned to her childhood love of painting. Her paintings were of scenes from the way life was when she was a child. Anna began painting seriously at the age of 78. In three decades she painted over 1,500 paintings. Her work initially sold for $3-$5, but as her fame increased her paintings went for $8,000 to $10,000.

During her life, Grandma Moses received critical acclaim. Her paintings were exhibited throughout the United States and Europe. In 1946, her work was being sold in the form of greeting cards.

She also published her autobiography, where she wrote, "I look back on my life like a good day's work. It was done, and I feel satisfied with it. I was happy and content. I knew nothing better and made the best out of what life offered. And life is what we make it, always has been, always will be." Grandma Moses died at the age of 101.[127]

There are endless stories like those above, but the most important are the ones that are yet to be written about your life. I have listed a few more examples for inspiration and motivation as you journey toward your destiny.

- Ronald Reagan & Donald Trump became President of the United States at 70.

- Janet Jackson had a baby at 50 while doing a world tour.

- Dr. Ruth Westheimer gained fame at the age of 53 as a sex expert, and continued to teach courses at Yale University into her 80's.

- Nelson Mandela became South Africa's oldest President at 74.

- Tim Zagat of restaurant guide fame, was 44 years old when he started the Zagat Restaurant Guide. When he was 51 years old in 1986, he left his job as a corporate lawyer for Gulf and Western Corporation.

- Believe it or not, the oldest Olympic champion, Oscar Swahn, won his 1st and 2nd gold medal when he was 60 years old in 1908, in the deer shooting competition (no deer were hurt). He returned to the Olympics in 1912 and won another gold medal. In 1920, he returned to the Olympics, and won the silver medal, holding the record as the oldest medalist in Olympic history. He was 72 years old at the time.

- Henry Ford introduced the Model T automobile when he was 45 years old. At the age of 60, he created the first car assembly line.

- Charles Darwin wrote the Origins of Species when he was 50 years old.

Retirement never occurs without trade-offs; it is not a zero sum game. Earlier in this book, I pointed out how self-assessment is the cornerstone to retiring and staying relevant. I emphasized that the psychological aspect of money and personal development plays a significant role in how they correlate to each other. Retirement doesn't mean giving up something, but trading in something for a residual benefit. Retirees often tell me the only luxury in life is time. So, now that you have time, how will you monetize your skills?

I began this chapter speaking about money. With money along, things are nice. With a skill or skills, life will always be better. I hope you now have a different perspective of how to value yourself more accurately because of the skills that you've been minimizing, or not maximizing, for far too long.

Tools and Worksheets:
Skill Monetization

WHAT WE DO DURING A SINGLE DAY

What we do during a single day – and how we do it – becomes the foundation of our whole lifetime. For what is life but the sum of our days?

Let's assess how we are spending our days.

1. Get a blank sheet of paper and go into a quiet space.
2. Multiply your age x 8760 (This will give your current age in hours) 8760X _____ age = _____
3. Subtract that number from 665,760 if male or 709,560 if female (that's based on average lifespan).

I have _____ hours left to _____.

CARPE DIEM

U.S. expectancy in 2011 was 78.7 years, which is slightly below the OECD average of 80.1. For U.S. men, the average life expectancy is 76, while it's 81 for U.S. women. (At five years, this gap in life expectancy between men and women is smaller than the OECD average of six years) as of Nov 21, 2013. Note: I'm optimistic through and through, but no one has ever gotten out alive. A person who doesn't worry about dying is a person too busy living.

How many vacations to do you take per year? _____ x _____ (number years). *Example: 1 vacation per year x 20 year lifespan = 20 more vacations. *Don't miss them.*

You can use this formula for any activity to make sure you maximize your days.

66 DAYS OF DAILY ACTIONS FOR
STAYING RELEVANT

DAY 1 OF 66

A #2 pencil and a dream can take you anywhere. Joyce Meyer

FINANCIAL	SPIRTUAL
I WANT	I BELIEVE
_____	_____
_____	_____
_____	_____
I WILL	I COMMIT
_____	_____
_____	_____
_____	_____
I DID	I MEDITATED ON
_____	_____
_____	_____
_____	_____

EMOTIONAL	PHYSICAL
I FELL	I WILL WORKOUT
I'M FOCUSED	I COMMIT
TODAY WAS	I DID

WHAT DO I WANT?

_____

_____

_____

_____

WHO DO I NEED TO BECOME TO GET IT?

_____

_____

_____

_____

SUMMARIZE YOUR ACTIVITIES OF THE DAY.

_____

_____

_____

_____

_____

_____

_____

_____

SEEK MENTORSHIP

The most impactful person outside of your parents will be the mentors throughout your life. A mentor hopes that you accomplish things that only they dreamed about. Mentors are self-actualized individuals with no need for anything but willing to give everything. The mentor and mentee relationship can be very powerful if done correctly. "Many people are looking for a mentor. But very few people are looking for someone to become a student to. I hope you catch that. It's easy to look for someone to pour into you. The hard decision is saying to oneself, I am ready to be the student to the right teacher." Mr.Buggs.

The list below outlines five different mentors because one person cannot be all things to one person. Remember we all have our strong suits and if you believe or your mentor tells you they are strong in everything, I would questions the value of their mentorship. Find someone that's confident enough in themselves to tell you the truth about you and themselves also.

Personal Mentor	This is someone who appears to model the lifestyle and core values that you would like to emulate.	Name: Name: Name:

Business or Corporate Mentor	This person has become one of the best in his/her industry and is well respected in and outside the boardroom.	Name: Name: Name:
Spiritual Mentor	This person does not speak about church or quote scriptures but they reflect the virtues of god and present you a truthful picture of what it means to be spiritual "not just on Sunday"	Name: Name: Name:
Emotional Mentor	This is your confidant, someone you can trust to tell you the truth no what, but will not judge or repeat your conversation.	Name: Name: Name:
Health Mentor	This person is spiritually, emotionally and physically in shape. They can provide you health tips, life lessons and	Name: Name: Name:

	positive energy. A personal mentor and health mentor are similar but different in that you don't talk about anything deep.	

*Virtual Mentorship can also be a viable option. They can mentor you through their books or tapes. I recommend you approach these five individuals see if they would be interested in your becoming their student.

** You should write down three names in each category as most often 2 out of 3 people will be unable to commit or will simply not be interested at this time. Sometimes you must first be worthy of that mentor's time by doing the work and presenting yourself to them after you've made some progress or become better known in the industry or social circle.

THE BLUEPRINT

ONE PAGE BUSINESS PLAN for _____ (year)

VISION STATEMENTS:

Personal: (Write one to three sentences expressing your personal dream.)

_____

_____

_____

Business: (Write one to three sentences expressing your dream for your company.)

_____

_____

_____

Strategy: (In general, how will you move your business forward during _____?) (year)

_____

_____

_____

_____

_____

Goals: (What would you like to accomplish in _____?)

_____

_____

_____

_____

Circle the three goals you would most want to say you achieved in your business during _____ (year) **by January 1,** _____ (the next year)?

Reword each circled goal so that it is:
- Specific
- Measurable
- Time-bounded

Top 3 _____ **(year)**

By_____:_____

By_____:_____

By_____:_____

    date

Chapter 23

Social Networks and Social Security

"Friends are the siblings God never gave us."
— Mencius

Getting ready to take the plunge requires some homework. It may seem daunting and, let's face it, you'd probably enjoy reading the ingredients on the back of soup can rather than this chapter, but knowing this information well before retirement could save you penalties if you forget to do something at the right time.

Well-thought-out decisions need to be made at least a year before retirement to understand the government benefits to which you will have access as a retiree and to get acquainted with what government sources are available and what you need to do to take advantage of these services.

For some programs, a late sign up can entail penalties. Hopefully, this chapter will delineate some of the choices you need to make to help you feel confident when signing up for benefits.

Before we jump into the weeds, let's look at the flowers. We will tackle both social network and social security, and how they impact each other. Take a look at these findings from the Framingham Heart study:

Objectives: To evaluate whether happiness can spread from person to person and whether niches of happiness form within social networks.

Design: Longitudinal social network analysis.

Setting: Framingham Heart Study social network.

Participants: 4,739 individuals followed from 1983 to 2003.

Main outcome measures: Happiness measured with validated four-item scale; the broad array of attributes of social networks and diverse social ties.

Results: Clusters of happy and unhappy people are visible in the network, and the relationship between people's happiness extends up to three degrees of separation (for example, to the friends of one's friends' friends). Individuals who are surrounded by many happy people and those who are central in the network are more likely to become happy in the future. Longitudinal statistical models suggest that clusters of happiness result from the spread of happiness and not just a tendency for people to associate with similar individuals. A friend who lives within a mile (about 1.6 km) and who becomes happy, increases the probability that a person is happy by 25% (95% confidence interval 1% to 57%). Similar effects are seen in co-resident spouses (8%, 0.2% to 16%), siblings who live within a mile (14%, 1% to 28%), and next-door neighbors (34%, 7% to 70%). Effects are not seen between coworkers. The effect decays with time and with geographical separation.

Conclusions: People's happiness depends on the happiness of others with whom they are connected. This provides further justification for seeing happiness, like health, as a collective phenomenon.

A study from Brigham Young University has found that people who have close relationships with family, friends, or co-workers have a significantly lower risk of death –50% lower!

The study also found that "Having few friends or weak social ties to the community is just as harmful to health as being an alcoholic or smoking nearly a pack of cigarettes a day. Weak social ties are more harmful than not exercising and twice as risky as being obese, the researchers found."

Clinical professor of psychiatry Dr. Waldinger said, "In over 75 years, our study has shown that the people who fared the best were the people who leaned into relationships with family, with friends, and with community."[128] This is the formula for staying relevant.[129]

Your social network is just a reflection of relationships you collected and managed over time. This point is, the better your social network, the longer you will live and the longer you will collect social security benefits. Now off to the weeds, or heavy lifting, of social security benefits and the details surrounding them.[130]

Social Security

Social security is an inflation-adjusted income resource one of the few remaining sources of a lifetime. It can play a very impactful role in your cash flow maximization strategy throughout retirement. However the Pension Research Council study conducted in 2010 to determine the knowledge people have about the social security system, it was found that if graded, 34% of study participants would receive a D or F on concepts as to how Social Security is calculated and taxed and available benefit benefits. Even though 84% said they felt confident in their knowledge of social security. It's vital that you have a full grasp of how, what, and when you should leverage your social security income pool.

While conventional wisdom suggests that people should begin collecting their Social Security retirement benefits as soon as possible or that Social Security benefits are only for old people, both assumptions are misguided. Since historic medical breakthroughs are increasing longevity, waiting to collect social security may be more beneficial. When you choose to collect Social Security benefits can have a significant impact on your retirement and lifestyle. Your personal prospective, family history, and marital status all play a role in selecting the option most applicable to your unique set of circumstances.

Things to consider:

- What is your family history of longevity?

- Are you married? If so, what is the age difference between you and your spouse?

- Have you ever been divorced? If so, did any of your previous marriages last at least ten years?

- Do you plan to continue working?

- Do you have any minor or disabled children?

- Do you have dependent parents who might outlive you?

- Are you or your spouse eligible for a government pension? What does this mean for benefits?

Social Security is a U.S. government program providing money to retirees, the disabled, or the unemployed. For our purposes, we'll look at how this program affects retirees. In all probability, you've been paying for Social Security throughout your working life. Now it's time to reap the rewards.

Social Security is available to people when they turn 62 ½. According to the government, however, 62 ½ is not considered full retirement. If you retire at 62 ½, you will receive less money than if you wait to retire. The age of full retirement is now correlated to the year of your birth."[131]

YEAR OF BIRTH*	FULL RETIREMENT AGE
1938	65 and 2 months
1939	65 and 4 months
1940	65 and 6 months
1941	65 and 8 months

1942	65 and 10 months
1943-1954	66
1955	66 and 2 months
1956	66 and 4 months
1957	66 and 6 months
1958	66 and 8 months
1959	66 and 10 months
1960 and later	67

Medicare Busters: What You Don't Know Can Add Up

Here are four common misconceptions about Medicare, the federal government's health insurance program for people who are aged 65 and older, or disabled.

Myth 1: Medicare covers long-term care.
Reality: At least 70% of people over age 65 will need long-term care, according to the Centers for Medicare & Medicaid Services (CMS) in Baltimore, Md., which is the federal agency that runs Medicare. But Medicare doesn't pay for the custodial care that typically makes up a large part of long-term care needs and costs. Instead, Medicare benefits are limited mainly to brief rehabilitation stays in nursing facilities, according to "Medicare & You 2016."[132]

Myth 2: Medicare premiums are cheaper than what I've been paying for private health insurance.

Reality: If you worked for a large corporation, you might wind up paying higher premiums when you switch to Medicare in retirement. It will almost certainly seem more complicated.

Myth 3: Now that Medicare provides drug coverage, my medication expenses will be lower in retirement than when I was working.

Reality: It depends on how generous your workplace benefits were. If you use traditional Medicare coverage, which includes Part A, Part B, and possibly supplemental coverage, you would also need Medicare Part D to get the bulk of your drug coverage. If you instead use a Medicare Advantage plan, it may or may not include drug coverage. But Medicare Part D has its premium, deductible, copayments and a coverage gap. And drug costs can vary depending on which medications you use, the plan you choose, whether you go to a pharmacy in your plan's network, and whether the drugs you use are on your plan's drug list, according to CMS.[133]

Myth 4: The age for starting Medicare is anytime after I turn 65 and decide to sign up.

Reality: You can postpone signing up for Medicare if you are covered under a group health plan based on current employment (your own, your spouse's, or a family member's if you're disabled). But if you don't have group health coverage, and you didn't sign up for Medicare when you were first eligible, you can only sign up in a specified window each year between January 1 and March 31. Your coverage would not start until July 1 of that year. Also, you may have to pay higher premiums for late enrollment in Medicare. [134]

Breaking Down Medicare

Although Social Security is available to people who turn 62 ½, Medicare does not begin until age 65. Essentially, there's a 5-year gap if you retire when you are eligible for Social Security. This means you will have to self-finance healthcare for at least five years. Consider retiring later if this is an option.

Getting older, even with Medicare is not cheap. Medicare is divided into different parts, each with different coverage. Trying to figure what it all means can be confusing. This chapter will, hopefully, help you through the fog.

Part A: Hospitalization

Part A basically covers inpatient hospital care, homecare in some circumstances, custodial care if there is some underlying medical condition, and hospice care. This is free if you are already receiving benefits from Social Security.[135]

With Part A you have your choice of doctors, hospitals, and other providers that accept Medicare. You pay a deductible and coinsurance (co-pay) for your Part A.[136]

You usually don't pay a monthly premium for Medicare Part A (Hospital Insurance) coverage if you or your spouse paid Medicare taxes while working. This is sometimes called "premium-free Part A." In other words, if you paid into Medicare, you now get the benefit of your tax dollars.

There are a few circumstances when a monthly premium is charged, so use the Medicare.gov calculator to find out if you will need to pay a premium at medicare.gov/eligibilitypremium calc.[137]

Be aware of the late enrollment penalty. If you don't sign up for Medicare Part A when you are first eligible, your monthly premium may go up 10%, and you'll have to pay the higher premium for twice the number of years you could have had Part A, if you had signed up.

That's a hefty fee.

For most people Medicare Part A eligibility is at 65 years of age, but check with Medicare.gov to verify when you need to sign up.[138]

Part B: Medical Insurance

Medicare Part B is medical insurance that covers services and supplies to treat a specific health condition. Services include outpatient care, medical equipment, limited physical therapy or rehabilitative services, preventative health services and screenings.[139] Unlike Part A, Part B has a premium. As of 2016, the standard Part B premium amount was $121.80 per month (or higher depending on your income). Part A and Part B Medicare are also referred to as Original Medicare.[140]

Part C: Supplemental Insurance

Supplemental Insurance, also referred to as Medigap, is what it sounds like: A supplemental policy that helps pay some of the healthcare costs that Original Medicare doesn't cover, such as copayments, coinsurance, and deductibles. Prescription drugs may also be covered. Supplemental policies are sold through private companies. To qualify you need to be enrolled in Medicare Part A and B.[141]

Part D: Prescription Drugs

Medicare offers prescription drug coverage to everyone with

Medicare. If you decide not to join a Medicare Prescription Drug Plan (Part D) when you're first eligible, or if you decide not to join a Medicare Advantage Plan Part C (like an HMO or PPO) or other Medicare health plan that offers Medicare prescription drug coverage, you are likely to pay a late enrollment penalty. This means a higher premium when you do sign up for drug coverage, whether you decide on Part D or a supplemental.[142]

Each Medicare Advantage Plan can charge different out-of-pocket costs and have different rules for how you get services (like whether you need a referral to see a specialist or if you have to go to specified doctors, facilities, or suppliers. You may also be required to use an Urgent Care facility for non-emergency or non-urgent care situations). These rules can change each year. Premiums vary with policies, so do your research.[143]

If you join a Medicare Advantage Plan, you still have Medicare. You'll get your Medicare Part A (Hospital Insurance) and Medicare Part B (Medical Insurance) coverage from the Medicare Advantage Plan and not Original Medicare.

Out-of-Pocket Health Costs
Just like the insurance you had before retiring, Medicare has out-of-pocket expenses to take into account. The following chart lists the out-of-pocket expenses associated with Medicare.[144]

Part A Premium
Most people don't pay a monthly premium for Part A. If you have less than ten years of working you will need to pay a premium since you have not contributed enough funds to the Medicare program. In 2017 the premium for Part A was up to $411 each month.

Part B Premium

In 2017 most people paid $134 each month (or more, depending on income). However, most people who get Social Security benefits will pay less than this amount ($109 on average).[145]

Part B deductible coinsurance

The deductible in 2017 was $183. After your deductible is met, you typically pay 20% of the Medicare-approved amount for most doctor services (including while you're a hospital inpatient), outpatient therapy, and for durable medical equipment, such as a walker, wheelchair, or hospital bed that is ordered by your doctor for use in the home.[146]

Keep in mind that Medicare does not pay for everything. If you need certain services Medicare doesn't cover; you'll have to pay for them yourself unless you have other insurance.

Some of the items and services that Medicare doesn't cover include:

- Long-term care
- Most dental care
- Eye examinations related to prescribing glasses
- Dentures
- Cosmetic surgery
- Acupuncture
- Hearing aids and exams for fitting them
- Routine foot care[147]

Tools and Worksheets:
Social Networks and Social Security

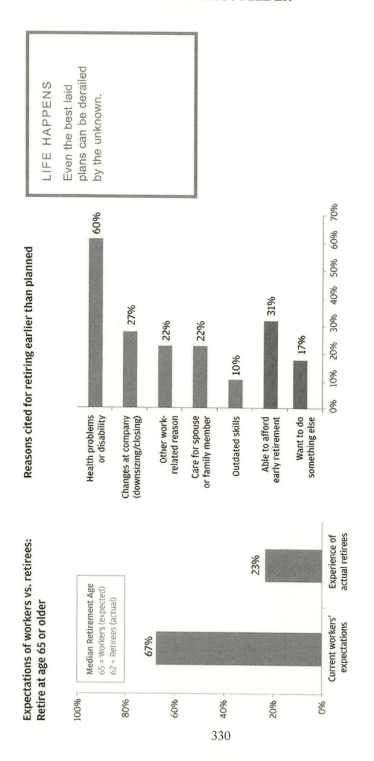

LIFE HAPPENS
Even the best laid plans can be derailed by the unknown.

Reasons cited for retiring earlier than planned

- Health problems or disability: 60%
- Changes at company (downsizing/closing): 27%
- Other work-related reason: 22%
- Care for spouse or family member: 22%
- Outdated skills: 10%
- Able to afford early retirement: 31%
- Want to do something else: 17%

Expectations of workers vs. retirees: Retire at age 65 or older

Median Retirement Age
65 = Workers (expected)
62 = Retirees (actual)

- Current workers' expectations: 67%
- Experience of actual retirees: 23%

Source: Employee Benefit Research Institute, Mathew Greenwald & Associates, Inc., 2015 Retirement Confidence Survey, Data as of March 2015.

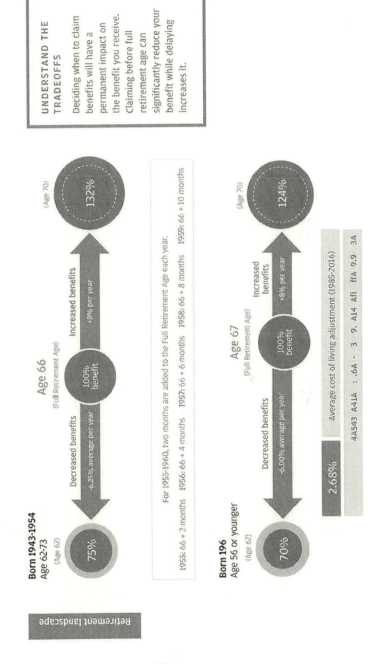

Social Security timing tradeoffs

Retirement landscape

Born 1943-1954
Age 62-73

(Age 62)
75%

Age 66
(Full Retirement Age)

100% benefit

(Age 70)
132%

Decreased benefits
-6.25% average per year

Increased benefits
+8% per year

UNDERSTAND THE TRADEOFFS

Deciding when to claim benefits will have a permanent impact on the benefit you receive. Claiming before full retirement age can significantly reduce your benefit while delaying increases it.

For 1955-1960, two months are added to the Full Retirement Age each year.

1955: 66 + 2 months   1956: 66 + 4 months   1957: 66 + 6 months   1958: 66 + 8 months   1959: 66 + 10 months

Born 196
Age 56 or younger

(Age 62)
70%

Age 67
(Full Retirement Age)

100% benefit

(Age 70)
124%

Decreased benefits
-6.00% average per year

Increased benefits
+8% per year

Average cost of living adjustment (1985-2016)

2.68%

4A543 A41A   : .6A -   3   9. A14 Afi fA 9,9   3A

331

What is Medicare?

Medicare is a government health care program available to those who have paid Medicare taxes while working or to non-working spouses of such individuals. Medicare is available when these individuals reach age 65. itizens who have never paid Medicare taxes may be eligible if they pay a Medicare premium. Individuals under age 65 may also be eligible if they are considered disabled by Social Security or the Railroad Retirement Board for more than 4 months.

	Traditional Medicare	Medicare Advantage (usually limited to a network of providers)
Part A: inpatient hospital insurance	✓	✓
Part B: doctors, tests and outpatient hospital insurance	✓	✓
Medigap: standardized plans that cover Part A and Part B co-pays and deductibles	✓	Not available
Part D: prescription drug insurance	✓	Most plans include Part D
Prescription drug co-pays and deductibles	Not covered	Not covered
Most vision dental and hearing expenses	Not covered	Coverage varies by plan
Long-term care	Not covered	Not covered

Reference

332

65 and working: Should I sign up for Medicare?

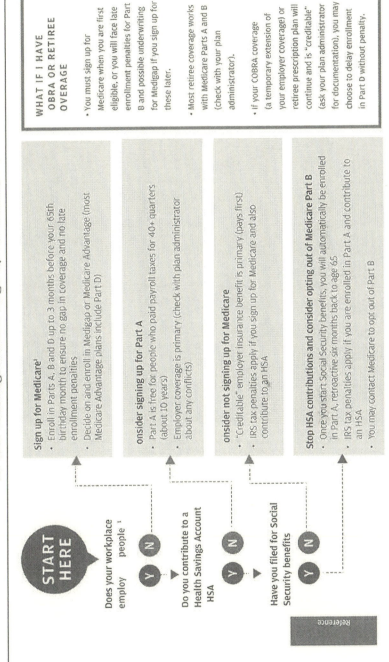

START HERE

Does your workplace employ people [1]   Y / N

Do you contribute to a Health Savings Account HSA   Y / N

Have you filed for Social Security benefits   Y / N

Sign up for Medicare[1]
- Enroll in Parts A, B and D up to 3 months before your 65th birthday month to ensure no gap in coverage and no late enrollment penalties
- Decide on and enroll in Medigap or Medicare Advantage (most Medicare Advantage plans include Part D)

Consider signing up for Part A
- Part A is free for people who paid payroll taxes for 40+ quarters (about 10 years)
- Employer coverage is primary (check with plan administrator about any conflicts)

Consider not signing up for Medicare
- "Creditable" employer insurance benefit is primary (pays first)
- IRS tax penalties apply if you sign up for Medicare and also contribute to an HSA

Stop HSA contributions and consider opting out of Medicare Part B
- Once you start Social Security benefits, you will automatically be enrolled in Part A, retroactive six months back to age 65
- IRS tax penalties apply if you are enrolled in Part A and contribute to an HSA
- You may contact Medicare to opt out of Part B

WHAT IF I HAVE COBRA OR RETIREE COVERAGE
- You must sign up for Medicare when you are first eligible, or you will face late enrollment penalties for Part B and possible underwriting for Medigap if you sign up for these later.
- Most retiree coverage works with Medicare Parts A and B (check with your plan administrator).
- If your COBRA coverage (a temporary extension of your employer coverage) or retiree prescription plan will continue and is "creditable" (ask your plan administrator for documentation), you may choose to delay enrollment in Part D without penalty.

Reference

333

Conclusion

"Gratitude makes sense of our past, brings peace for today, and creates a vision for tomorrow."
— Melody Beattie

I would like to again thank you for taking the time to read a portion, or even my entire book. This project was my way of staying relevant and sharing my unique perspective on life and money management. I believe in the power of words, so I hope that my desire to have at least 1 -10 million people read my book will happen in my lifetime. Let's recap in a few paragraphs what it took me hundreds of pages to communicate.

First, without understanding how you think and why you think the thoughts that you think, you will never be able to become or stay relevant. The prerequisite for significance is relevance, so it begins with knowing how you want to be relevant in the future.

Secondly, you must know your numbers because what is measured multiplies. The numbers are very significant because they always change, but with change comes progress. Next, you have to apply what I've shared within sixty-six days of reading this book. As you now know, new research has shown it takes sixty-six days to create a sustainable habit.

I said in my introduction that I wrote this book so that it would be like the Bible, helping you through all phases of life. Remember, I want you to put this book next to your word of faith (whatever that may be). The next time you go awhile without reading both books, you will know you are heading in the wrong direction. This book is meant to be used as a lifelong resource. Obviously investment limits and investment options will change but what remains constant is that the only person that can ensure that you stay relevant is you. Staying relevant is much bigger than money or things. Staying relevant allows you to fully engage in the now so that you will be even more relevant in the future.

I hope this book has provided a wake-up call for some, enlightenment for others, or confirmation for what many already knew. My deepest desire is that I have reached you in a way that no other retirement or self-help material has in the past. Thanks again for helping me stay relevant. I hope this book will help you stay relevant before, during, and after retirement.

Acknowledgements

I'd like to thank my clients for putting their trust in me and sharing their stories. They have given me the reason to write this book as a guide for their retirement planning.

Thank you to my family, for enduring the hours I've spent poring over information and writing this book.

Thank you also, to Lori Wark and Gina Hagler, for their willingness to read each draft of this book in progress, and the suggestions they offered for making it even stronger.

Glossary for Business Owners

Please download glossary at:
www.holisticplanners.com

Glossary for Individuals

Please download glossary at:
www.holisticplanners.com

Resources by Age

Please download Resources by Age at:
www.holisticplanners.com

Endnotes

[1] Skills, The, Expertise Of Fund Managers Are Supposed To Give Them The Ability To Select Better Stocks, and Bonds than an Index like the Dow or S&P 500. "86% of active managers failed to beat the market in 2014." CNNMoney. *Accessed May 11, 2017.* http://money.cnn.com/2015/03/12/investing/investing-active-versus-passive-funds/index.html.

[2] Lauren Gensler, Warren Buffett Slams Wall Street, Says $100 Billion Wasted on Investment Fees, https://www.forbes.com/sites/laurengensler/2017/02/25/warren-buffett-annual-letter-2016-passive-active-investing/#767c3173286b, *retrieved May 11, 2017.*

[3] Novack, Janet. "6 Pointed Questions To Ask Before Hiring A Financial Advisor." Forbes. June 30, 2015. *Accessed May 24, 2017.* https://www.forbes.com/sites/janetnovack/2013/09/20/6-pointed-questions-to-ask-before-hiring-a-financial-advisor/#1bb01395489f, retrieved May 9, 2017.

[4] Starecheski, Laura. "Why Saying Is Believing - The Science Of Self-Talk." NPR. October 07, 2014. *Accessed May 2, 2017.* http://www.npr.org/sections/health-shots/2014/10/07/353292 408/why-saying-is-believing-the-science-of-self-talk.

[5] Ibid.

[6] Lally, Phillippa, Van Jaarsveld Cornelia H. M., Henry W. W. Potts, and Jane Wardle. "How are habits formed: Modelling habit formation in the real world." European Journal of Social Psychology. July 16, 2009. *Accessed May 24, 2017.* http://onlineli brary.wiley.com/doi/10.1002/ejsp.674/abstract, *Accessed May 21, 2017.*

[7] "Jim Rohn on Action Vs. Self Delusion." Tom2tall. http://www.tom2tall.com/Jim-Rohn-Action-versus-Delusion.html, *Accessed, May 6, 2017.*

[8] A quote by Benjamin Franklin." Goodreads. *Accessed June 14, 2017.* https://www.goodreads.com/quotes/409087-there-are-t wo-ways-to-increase-your-wealth-increase-your.

[9] "What Is NeuroFinance?" Elise Payzan-LeNestour. November 12, 2015. *Accessed May 24, 2017.* http://www.elisepayzan.c om/neurofinance-definition, *Accessed May 2, 2017.*

[10] ParisTech Review." Understanding the financial brain: the goal of neuroeconomics. *Accessed May 24, 2017.* http://www.pa ristechreview.com/2010/05/17/understanding-the-financial-brain-the-goal-of-neuroeconomics.

[11] Tom, Pamela. "Neuroeconomics: Studying Brain Responses Gives Marketers Increased Ability to Predict How People Make Decisions." Haas News | Berkeley-Haas. April 21, 2017. *Accessed May 24, 2017.* http://newsroom.haas.berkeley.edu/rese arch-news/neuroeconomics-studying-brain-responses-gives-m arketers-increased-ability-predict-how.

[12] National Center for Responsible Gaming, Increasing the Odds, Gambling and the Brain: Why Neuroscience Research is Vital to Gambling Research. 2011. *Accessed December 3, 2016.* http://www.ncrg.org/sites/default/files/uploads/docs/monograp hs/ncrgmonograph6final.pdf

[13] "Where will my retirement income come from?" Sources of Retirement Income - Fidelity. June 05, 2017. *Accessed June 15, 2017.* https://www.fidelity.com/viewpoints/retirement/retireme nt-income-sources.

[14] Ibid.

[15] Lubin, Gus. "Cuban On Investing: Diversification Is For Idiots." Business Insider. August 13, 2011. *Accessed May 24, 2017.* http://www.businessinsider.com/cuban-on-investing-diversifica tion-is-for-idiots-2011-8, *Accessed May 10, 2017.*

[16] Where will my retirement income come from?" Sources of Retirement Income - Fidelity. March 02, 2017. *Accessed May 24, 2017.* https://www.fidelity.com/viewpoints/retirement/retir ement-income-sources.

[17] Gallup, Inc. "Average U.S. Retirement Age Rises to 62." Gallup.com. April 28, 2014. *Accessed May 24, 2017.* http://www .gallup.com/poll/168707/average-retirement-age-rises.aspx,

[18] "Briefs." Center for Retirement Research. *Accessed June 15, 2017.* http://crr.bc.edu/briefs/the-average-retirement-age-an-u pdate/.

[19] "The math of retirement savings." Retirement Guidelines - Fidelity. June 05, 2017. *Accessed June 15, 2017.* https://www.fide lity.com/viewpoints/retirement/retirement-guidelines.

[20] Ibid.

[21] The savings factor, savings rate, and withdrawal rate targets are based on simulations based on historical market data. These simulations take into account the volatility that a variety of asset allocations might be experienced under different market conditions. Given the above assumptions for retirement age, planning age, wage growth, and income replacement targets, the results were successful in nine out of 10 hypothetical market conditions where the average equity allocation over the investment horizon was more than 50% for the hypothetical portfolio. Remember, past performance is no guarantee of future results. Performance returns for actual investments will generally be reduced by fees or expenses not reflected in these hypothetical calculations. Returns will also generally be reduced by taxes.

The income replacement rate is the percentage of preretirement income that an individual should target to replace in retirement. The income replacement targets are based on a Consumer Expenditure Survey 2011 (BLS), Statistics of Income 2011 Tax State, IRS 2014 tax brackets, and Social Security Benefit Calculators. The 45% income replacement target assumes no pension income, and a retirement and Social Security claiming age of 67, which is the full Social Security benefit age for those born in 1960 or later. For an earlier retirement and claiming age, this target goes up due to lower Social Security retirement benefits. Similarly, the target goes down for a later retirement age. For a retirement age of 65, this target is defined as 50% of preretirement annual income, and for a retirement age of 70, this target is defined as 40% of preretirement income.

The savings factor is a multiple of income that an individual should aim to have saved by a given age. For example, you should aim to have saved 1x your current income by age 30. Fidelity developed a series of income multiplier targets corresponding to different ages, assuming a retirement age of 67, a 15% savings rate, a 1.5% constant real wage growth, a planning age through 93, and an income replacement target of 45% of preretirement income (assumes no pension income). The final income multiplier is calculated to be 10x your preretirement income and assumes a retirement age of 67. For an earlier retirement age, this target goes up due to lower Social Security retirement benefits and a longer retirement horizon. Similarly, the target goes down for a later retirement age. For a retirement age of 65, this target is defined as 12x, and for a retirement age of 70, this target is defined as 8x.

Fidelity's suggested total pretax savings goal of 15% of annual income (including employer contributions) is based on

Fidelities' research, which indicates that most people would need to contribute this amount from an assumed starting age of 25 through an assumed retirement age of 67 to potentially support a replacement annual income rate equal to 45% of pre-retirement annual income (assuming no pension income) through age 93.

The sustainable withdrawal rate is defined as an inflation-adjusted annual withdrawal rate and expressed as a percentage of your initial (at retirement) savings balance. This rate is estimated to be 4.5%, assuming a retirement age of 67 and a planning age through 93.

Guidance is educational in nature, and is not individualized or intended to serve as the primary basis for your investment or tax-planning decisions. We encourage you to build a retirement plan based on your personal time horizon, risk tolerance, retirement goals, and financial situation.

The savings factor, savings rate, and withdrawal rate targets are hypothetical illustrations, do not reflect actual investment results, actual lifetime income, and are not guarantees of future results. Targets do not take into consideration the specific situation of any particular user, the composition of any particular account, or any particular investment or investment strategy. Individual users may need to save more or less than the illustrated targets depending on their retirement age, life expectancy, market conditions, desired retirement lifestyle, and other factors.

Source: Fidelity Investment

[22] Powell, Robert. "Scammers targeting your retirement funds." MarketWatch. October 23, 2013. *Accessed June 15, 2017.* http:/

/www.marketwatch.com/story/scammers-targeting-your-retire
ment-funds-2013-10-23.

[23] "Fact Sheet: Cash Balance Pension Plans." United States Department of Labor. July 27, 2016. *Accessed June 19, 2017.* http
s://www.dol.gov/agencies/ebsa/about-ebsa/our-activities/resour
ce-center/fact-sheets/cash-balance-pension-plans.

[24] "Wedding statistics in the United States." Wedding statistics
in the United States | SoundVision.com. *Accessed June 16, 2017.*
https://www.soundvision.com/article/wedding-statistics-in-the
-united-states.

[25] Divorce Rate in U.S. Drops to Nearly 40-Year Low." Time.
http://time.com/4575495/divorce-rate-nearly-40-year-low. *Accessed May 6, 2017.*

[26] "The National Average Cost of a Wedding Hits $35,329."
Theknot.com. *Accessed June 19, 2017.* https://www.theknot.com
/content/average-wedding-cost-2016.

[27] Woolston, M.S. Chris. "HealthDay." Current Health News.
January 20, 2017. *Accessed June 19, 2017.* https://consumer.healt
hday.com/encyclopedia/emotional-health-17/love-sex-and-rela
tionship-health-news-452/marriage-and-stress-645970.html.

[28] Finkel, Eli J. "Opinion | The All-or-Nothing Marriage." The
New York Times. February 14, 2014. *Accessed June 19, 2017.*
https://www.nytimes.com/2014/02/15/opinion/sunday/the-all-
or-nothing-marriage.html.

[29] "Mourning the Death of a Spouse." National Institute on Aging. July 11, 2011. *Accessed June 20, 2017.* https://www.nia.nih.gov/health/publication/mourning-death-spouse#what.

[30] Dolgen, Ellen. "Why More Women Are Staying Single." The Huffington Post. February 14, 2014. *Accessed June 16, 2017.* http://www.huffingtonpost.com/ellen-sarver-dolgen/why-more-women-are-staying-single_b_4783163.html.

[31] Pew Research Center, Social and Demographic Trends, Chapter 1: Women in Leadership, http://www.pewsocialtrends.org/2015/01/14/chapter-1-women-in-leadership, *retrieved May 10, 2017*

[32] Keefe, Joe. "Gender Equality As an Investment Concept."The Huffington Post. August 25, 2014. *Accessed March 24, 2017.* http://www.huffingtonpost.com/joe-keefe/gender-equality-as-an-inv_b_5700228.html.

[33] "Are You a Woman of Influence? Allianz Life Study Reveals Profile of More Financially Empowered Woman." Business Wire. July 15, 2013. *Accessed March 24, 2017.* http://www.businesswire.com/news/home/20130715005800/en/Woman-Influence-Allianz-Life-Study-Reveals-Profile.

[34] Cougar myth busted." News-Medical.net. August 18, 2010. *Accessed March 24, 2017.* http://www.news-medical.net/news/20100818/Cougar-myth-busted.aspx.

[35] Ibid.

[36] Blue, Laura. "Why Do Women Live Longer Than Men?" Time. August 06, 2008. *Accessed June 19, 2017.* http://content. time.com/time/health/article/0,8599,1827162,00.html.

[37] Long-Term Care in America: Expectations and Preferences for Care and Caregiving Research Highlights | Longtermcare poll.org | APNORC.org. *Accessed June 19, 2017.* http://www.lo ngtermcarepoll.org/pages/polls/long-term-care-in-america-exp ectations-and-preferences-for-care-and-caregiving-research-hi ghlights.aspx.

[38] "Pay Gap: Working Women With Kids Makes Less Money Vs. Men | Money." Time. *Accessed June 19, 2017.* http://time.co m/money/4097277/pay-gap-working-women-men-difference/

[39] Brown, Anna, and Eileen Patten. "The narrowing, but persistent, gender gap in pay." Pew Research Center. April 03, 2017. *Accessed June 19, 2017.* http://www.pewresearch.org/fact-tank/2017/04/03/gender-pay-gap-facts/.

[40] Ibid.

[41] Napoleon, Think and Grow Rich. New York: Penguin Random House, LLC, 2016. (Originally published in 1937).

[42] W. Bradford Wilcox, Nicholas H. Wolfinger. "Hey Guys, Put a Ring on It." National Review. February 09, 2017. *Accessed*

June 20, 2017. http://www.nationalreview.com/article/444746/marriage-benefits-men-take-note.

[43] Men and Marriage. Debunking the Ball and Chain. *Accessed June 19, 2017.* https://ifstudies.org/ifs-admin/resources/men-and-marriage-research-brief.pdf

[44] W. Bradford Wilcox, Nicholas H. Wolfinger. "Hey Guys, Put a Ring on It." National Review. February 09, 2017. *Accessed June 20, 2017.* http://www.nationalreview.com/article/444746/marriage-benefits-men-take-note.

[45] Ferri, Rick. "Firing Your Adviser is Easy." Forbes. June 26, 2012. *Accessed May 1, 2017.* https://www.forbes.com/sites/rickferri/2012/06/26/firing-your-adviser-is-easy/#459f97c86945.

[46] Morin, Rich, and Richard Fry. "More Americans Worry about Financing Retirement." Pew Research Center's Social & Demographic Trends Project. October 22, 2012. *Accessed June 20, 2017.* http://www.pewsocialtrends.org/2012/10/22/more-americans-worry-about-financing-retirement/.

[47] Bogert, Rachael. "Is 60 the New 40?" Chicagotribune.com. April 25, 2010. *Accessed June 19, 2017.* http://www.chicagotribune.com/sns-health-60-new-40-story.html.

[48] AgeWave: Boomers Taking Charge of Their Health. When I'm 64. *Accessed February 26, 2017.* https://mlaem.fs.ml.com/content/dam/ML/Articles/pdf/ml_health-and-retirement-planning-for-the-great-unknown.pdf.

[49] Ibid.

[50] Backman, Maurie. "Older Americans Are More Afraid of Running Out of Money Than Death." The Motley Fool. January 01, 1970. *Accessed June 19, 2017.* https://www.fool.com/retirement/2016/09/25/older-americans-are-more-afraid-of-running-out-of.aspx.

[51] Combined undergraduate and graduate debt by degree: Political Science Rumors. *Accessed June 19, 2017.* http://www.poliscirumors.com/topic/combined-undergraduate-and-graduate-debt-by-degree.

[52] Ibid.

[53] Agarwal, Shreya. "Homeownership Rates Are Falling, And It's Not Just A Millennial Problem." Forbes. May 06, 2016. *Accessed June 19, 2017.* https://www.forbes.com/sites/shreyaagarwal/2016/05/06/homeownership-rates-are-falling-and-its-not-just-a-millennial-problem/#29e718b3494a.

[54] Agarwal, Shreya. "Homeownership Rates Are Falling, And It's Not Just A Millennial Problem." Forbes. May 06, 2016. *Accessed June 19, 2017.* https://www.forbes.com/sites/shreyaagarwal/2016/05/06/homeownership-rates-are-falling-and-its-not-just-a-millennial-problem/#1d1c3e46494a.

[55] "Real Estate Investing: Risks and Benefits." Zillow Porchlight. December 06, 2015. *Accessed June 19, 2017.* https://www.zillow.com/blog/real-estate-investing-risks-and-benefits-128691/.

[56] Contributor, Guest, and Kathleen Burns Kingsbury. "Women must overcome retirement-saving roadblocks." CNBC. September 02, 2014. *Accessed June 19, 2017.* http://www.cnbc.com/20 14/06/16/women-face-retirement-roadblocks.html?view=story &%24DEVICE%24=native-android-tablet.

[57] Payne, Ruby K. A framework for understanding poverty: a cognitive approach. Highlands, TX: Aha! Process, Inc., 2013.

[58] To raise a child born in 2013 to the age of 18. "Average cost of raising a child hits $245,000." CNNMoney. *Accessed June 19, 2017.* http://money.cnn.com/2014/08/18/pf/child-cost/index.html.

[59] Parker, Kim, and Eileen Patten. "The Sandwich Generation." Pew Research Center's Social & Demographic Trends Project. January 29, 2013. *Accessed June 19, 2017.* http://www.pewsoci altrends.org/2013/01/30/the-sandwich-generation/.

[60] Daily, Investor's Business. "Eldercare: When Parents Need Help." Investor's Business Daily. *Accessed March 24, 2017.* Htt p://www.investors.com/promoted-content/blackrock/eldercare -when-parents-need-help.

[61] Daily, Investor's Business. "Eldercare: When Parents Need Help." Investor's Business Daily. *Accessed March 24, 2017.* http:/ /www.investors.com/promoted-content/blackrock/eldercare-w hen-parents-need-help/.

[62] "BlackRock Retirement Institute." BlackRock. *Accessed May 24, 2017.* https://www.blackrock.com/investing/retirement/bla ckrock-retirement-institute

[63] "BlackRock Retirement Institute." BlackRock. *Accessed May 24, 2017.* https://www.blackrock.com/investing/retirement/bla ckrock-retirement-institute

[64] Ibid.

[65] BlackRock Retirement Institute." BlackRock. *Accessed May 24, 2017.* https://www.blackrock.com/investing/retirement/bla ckrock-retirement-institute

[66] Ellis-Christensen, Tricia, and O. Wallace. "What Percent of the US Population do Doctors Comprise?" WiseGEEK. June 03, 2017. *Accessed June 19, 2017.* http://www.wisegeek.org/what -percent-of-the-us-population-do-doctors-comprise.htm.

[67] Rowell. "Estimated probability of competing in professional athletics." NCAA.org - The Official Site of the NCAA. March 13, 2017. *Accessed June 19, 2017.* http://www.ncaa.org/about/res ources/research/estimated-probability-competing-professional-athletics.

[68] India, Press Trust of. "50% of occupations today will no longer exist in 2025: Report." Business Standard. November 08, 2014. *Accessed June 19, 2017.* http://www.business-standard.com/artic le/pti-stories/50-of-occupations-today-will-no-longer-exist-in-2025-report-114110701279_1.html.

[69] Lake, Rebecca. "Television Statistics: 23 Mind-Numbing Facts to Watch." CreditDonkey. *Accessed June 19, 2017.* https://www.creditdonkey.com/television-statistics.html.

[70] "Income from Pensions." Income from Pensions | Pension Rights Center. January 05, 2011. *Accessed June 19, 2017.* http://www.pensionrights.org/publications/statistic/income-pensions.

[71] Ibid.

[72] Ibid.

[73] "Pension Rights Center." Pension Rights Center. *Accessed June 20, 2017.* http://www.pensionrights.org/.

[74] Ibid.

[75] Rank, Mark R. "Opinion | From Rags to Riches to Rags." The New York Times. April 18, 2014. *Accessed June 23, 2017.* https://www.nytimes.com/2014/04/20/opinion/sunday/from-rags-to-riches-to-rags.html?smid=pl-share.

[76] Ibid.

[77] Ibid.

[78] "Welcome to NEFE." National Endowment for Financial Education | NEFE. *Accessed June 23, 2017.* http://nefe.org/.

[79] "MMC Institute." MMC Institute Sudden Wealth Syndrome Comments. *Accessed June 23, 2017.* http://www.mmcinstitute.com/about-2/sudden-wealth-syndrome/.

[80] Chandra C. Gray, The Post World War II Era American Dream Home and Its Influence on the Homes of Today. May 2000, https://ttu-ir.tdl.org/ttu-ir/bitstream/handle/2346/23203/31295014859382.pdf?sequence=1, *retrieved May 23, 2017.*

[81] Tankersley, Jim. "Economic mobility hasn't changed in a half-century in America, economists declare." The Washington Post. January 23, 2014. *Accessed June 25, 2017.* https://www.washingtonpost.com/business/economy/economic-mobility-hasnt-changed-in-a-half-century-in-america-economists-declare/2014/01/22/e845db4a-83a2-11e3-8099-9181471f7aaf_story.html?utm_term=.a11ef33f8264.

[82] Sowell, Thomas. Wealth, poverty, and politics. New York: Basic Books, 2016.

[83] Payne, Ruby K. *A framework for understanding poverty: a cognitive approach.* Highlands, TX: Aha! Process, Inc., 2013.

[84] Ibid.

[85] Steinsaltz, David. "Will 90 Become The New 60?" Aging on Nautilus. March 06, 2017. *Accessed June 25, 2017.* http://aging.nautil.us/feature/176/will-90-become-the-new-60.

[86] "DETERMINED." Ernestine Shepherd. *Accessed June 25, 2017.* http://ernestineshepherd.net/?page_id=2.

[87] Longman, Jeré. "85-Year-Old Marathoner Is So Fast That Even Scientists Marvel." The New York Times. December 28, 2016. *Accessed June 25, 2017.* https://www.nytimes.com/2016/12/28/sports/ed-whitlock-marathon-running.html.

[88] Steinsaltz, David. "Will 90 Become The New 60?" Aging on Nautilus. March 06, 2017. *Accessed June 25, 2017.* http://aging.nautil.us/feature/176/will-90-become-the-new-60.

[89] Merrill Lynch/Age Wave. The New Social Security: Strong Relationships Matter. *Accessed March 19, 2017.* http://www.ml.com/retirementstudys, P. 15.

[90] "Growing Awareness of a Senior Epidemic." Start page. *Accessed June 25, 2017.* http://www.caringnews.com/en/166/1/430/Growing-Awareness-of-a-Senior-Epidemic.htm.

[91] Ibid.

[92] "Landmark Research and Consulting." Age Wave. *Accessed June 25, 2017.* http://agewave.com/what-we-do/landmark-research-and-consulting/research-studies/leisure-in-retirement-beyond-the-bucket-list/.

[93] Ibid.

[94] Knickman, James R., and Emily K. Snell. "The 2030 Problem: Caring for Aging Baby Boomers." Health Services Research. August 2002. *Accessed June 25, 2017*. https://www.ncbi.nlm.nih.gov/pmc/articles/PMC1464018/.

[95] Ibid.

[96] "Long Term Care Costs 2016." Genworth. *Accessed June 25, 2017*. https://www.genworth.com/about-us/industry-expertise/cost-of-care.html.

[97] "Medicaid Eligibility." Medicaid Eligibility - Long-Term Care Information. *Accessed June 25, 2017*. https://longtermcare.acl.gov/medicare-medicaid-more/medicaid/medicaid-eligibility

[98] Botek, Anne-Marie, Rodneyfisher, and Karenlorenzo. "Turning to 'Shared Care' for Cheaper Long-Term Care Insurance." Shared Long-Term Care Insurance for Couples - AgingCare.com. July 06, 2012. *Accessed June 25, 2017*. https://www.agingcare.com/articles/shared-long-term-care-insurance-151804.htm.

[99] " Long-term Care Considerations for LGBT Adults." Long-term Care Considerations for LGBT Adults - Long-Term Care Information. Accessed June 25, 2017. https://longtermcare.acl.gov/the-basics/lgbt/.

[100] "Facing up to the costs of long-term care." CNNMoney. Accessed June 25, 2017. http://money.cnn.com/2007/10/22/pf/long_term_insurance.moneymag/index.htm.

[101] National Institute on Aging. *Accessed June 25, 2017.* https://www.nia.nih.gov/alzheimers/publication/alzheimers-disease-fact-sheet.

[102] "Latest Alzheimer's Facts and Figures." Latest Facts & Figures Report | Alzheimer's Association. March 29, 2016. *Accessed June 25, 2017.* http://www.alz.org/facts/.

[103] Ibid.

[104] "Squared Away Blog." Img_header_squaredawayblog. *Accessed June 25, 2017.* http://squaredawayblog.bc.edu/squared-away/5-signs-of-financial-impairment/.

[105] Ibid.

[106] Ibid.

[107] About Alzheimer's Disease: Symptoms." National Institute on Aging. February 25, 2014. *Accessed June 25, 2017.* https://www.nia.nih.gov/alzheimers/topics/symptoms.

[108] Ibid.

[109] Ibid.

[110] The NIH Alzheimer's Disease Education and Referral Center offers more information on getting a diagnosis and latest methods for diagnosis. NIH also provides a list of research fa-

cilities across the country. The Mayo Clinic's Alzheimer's resources provide an overview of various tests doctors may perform in their office, or order to be done in a separate appointment. The Alzheimer's Association has information on finding a physician and the steps physicians will take during medical evaluation.

[111] "Getting Your Affairs in Order." National Institute on Aging. July 11, 2011. *Accessed June 20, 2017.* https://www.nia.nih.gov /health/publication/getting-your-affairs-order.

[112] Ibid.

[113] Ibid.

[114] "Getting Your Affairs in Order." National Institute on Aging. July 11, 2011. *Accessed June 20, 2017.* https://www.nia.nih.gov /health/publication/getting-your-affairs-order.

[115] "Understanding the Medicaid "Look-Back" and "Transfer Penalty" Rules - St. Louis, MO | Coulson Elder Law." Estate Planning and Elder Law Attorney | Coulson Elder Law. August 16, 2016. *Accessed June 20, 2017.* http://coulsonelderlaw.com/u nderstanding-medicaid-lookback-transfer-penalty-rules.

[116] "The Latest in Nutrition Related Research." NutritionFacts .org. *Accessed June 20, 2017.* https://nutritionfacts.org/.

[117] "Retiree health costs rise." Retiree Health Costs Rise – Fidelity. August 16, 2016. *Accessed June 20, 2017.* https://www.fi delity.com/viewpoints/retirement/retiree-health-costs-rise.

[118] Ibid.

[119] "Older Adults." Choose MyPlate. November 16, 2016. *Accessed June 20, 2017.* https://www.choosemyplate.gov/older-adults.

[120] "Hip Fractures Among Older Adults." Centers for Disease Control and Prevention. September 20, 2016. *Accessed March 1, 2017.* https://www.cdc.gov/homeandrecreationalsafety/falls/ad ulthipfx.html.

[121] Interview with Meredith Mickelson, MS, June 19, 2017. http://meredithmickelson.com/

[122] Appendix 1. Physical Activity Guidelines for Americans - 2015-2020 Dietary Guidelines. 2008. *Accessed February 23, 2017.* https://health.gov/dietaryguidelines/2015/guidelines/appendix -1/.

[123] Ibid.

[124] "Colonel Harland Sanders." Biography.com. April 28, 2017. *Accessed June 20, 2017.* https://www.biography.com/people/colo nel-harland-sanders-12353545.

[125] "J.C. Penney." Biography.com. April 02, 2014. *Accessed June 20, 2017.* https://www.biography.com/people/jc-penney-38638.

[126] Lee, Hermione. Penelope Fitzgerald: a life. New York: Vintage Books, a division of Penguin Random House LLC, 2015.

[127] "National Museum of Women in the Arts." Grandma Moses (Anna Mary Robertson Moses) | National Museum of Women in the Arts. *Accessed June 20, 2017.* https://nmwa.org/explore/artist-profiles/grandma-moses-anna-mary-robertson-moses.

[128] O'Connor, Anahad. "The Secrets to a Happy Life, From a Harvard Study." The New York Times. March 23, 2016. *Accessed June 20, 2017.* https://well.blogs.nytimes.com/2016/03/23/the-secrets-to-a-happy-life-from-a-harvard-study/.

[129] Fowler, James H., and Nicholas A. Christakis. "Dynamic spread of happiness in a large social network: longitudinal analysis over 20 years in the Framingham Heart Study." BMJ. December 05, 2008. *Accessed June 25, 2017.* http://www.bmj.com/content/337/bmj.a2338.

[130] "Framingham Heart Study." Framingham Heart Study. *Accessed June 20, 2017.* https://www.framinghamheartstudy.org/.

[131] "Social Security." Full Retirement Age. *Accessed June 20, 2017.* https://www.ssa.gov/planners/retire/retirechart.html.

[132] "Medicare and Your 2026." *Accessed June 19, 2017.* https://www.medicare.gov/pubs/pdf/10050.pdf.

[133] Ibid.

[134] Ibid.

[135] "What Is Medicare Part A?" Medicare Insurance Options from eHealth Medicare. Accessed June 20, 2017. https://www.ehealthmedicare.com/about-medicare/medicare-part-a.

[136] "Your Medicare coverage choices." Medicare.gov - the Official U.S. Government Site for Medicare. *Accessed June 20, 2017.* https://www.medicare.gov/sign-up-change-plans/decide-how-to-get-medicare/your-medicare-coverage-choices.html#collapse-3134.

[137] Medicare.gov - Eligibility & Premium Calculator. *Accessed June 20, 2017.* https://www.medicare.gov/eligibilitypremiumcalc.

[138] "What Part A covers." Medicare.gov - the Official U.S. Government Site for Medicare. *Accessed June 20, 2017.* https://www.medicare.gov/what-medicare-covers/part-a/what-part-a-covers.html.

[139] "What Part B covers." Medicare.gov - the Official U.S. Government Site for Medicare. *Accessed June 20, 2017.* https://www.medicare.gov/what-medicare-covers/part-b/what-medicare-part-b-covers.html.

[140] "Part B costs." Medicare.gov - the Official U.S. Government Site for Medicare. *Accessed June 20, 2017.* https://www.medicare.gov/your-medicare-costs/part-b-costs/part-b-costs.html.

[141] "What's Medicare Supplement Insurance (Medigap)?" Medicare.gov - the Official U.S. Government Site for Medicare.

Accessed June 20, 2017. https://www.medicare.gov/supplement-other-insurance/medigap/whats-medigap.html.

[142] "Medigap & Medicare drug coverage (Part D)." Medicare.gov - the Official U.S. Government Site for Medicare. *Accessed June 20, 2017.* https://www.medicare.gov/supplement-other-insurance/medigap/medigap-and-part-d/medigap-plans -and-part-d.html.

[143] "Costs for Medicare Advantage Plans." Medicare.gov - the Official U.S. Government Site for Medicare. *Accessed June 20, 2017.* https://www.medicare.gov/your-medicare-costs/medicar e-health-plan-costs/costs-for-medicare-advantage-plans.html.

[144] "Medicare 2017 costs at a glance." Medicare.gov - the Official U.S. Government Site for Medicare. *Accessed June 25, 2017.* https://www.medicare.gov/your-medicare-costs/costs-at-a-gla nce/costs-at-glance.html.

[145] "Part B costs." Medicare.gov - the Official U.S. Government Site for Medicare. *Accessed June 25, 2017.* https://www.medicar e.gov/your-medicare-costs/part-b-costs/part-b-costs.html.

[146] Ibid.

[147] "What Part A & Part B doesn't cover." Medicare.gov - the Official U.S. Government Site for Medicare. *Accessed June 25, 2017.* https://www.medicare.gov/what-medicare-covers/not-co vered/item-and-services-not-covered-by-part-a-and-b.html.

[148] Retirement reimagined: How Baby Boomers can plan for an active retirement." Baby Boomers can plan for an active retirement. December 08, 2016. *Accessed February 12, 2017.* https://www.chase.com/news/120616-retirement-reimagined.

[149] Tory through all the criticism and critiques I know you just want me to become the best version of me. I hope that one day all the ups and downs will be a footnote in a life full of moments that were worth all the pain and sacrifice that you made for the kids and me. You said you didn't want a dreamer or a person that doesn't finish or produce; well this is the first step to our dreams. I don't want to be a footnote in your life, but I want to stay relevant. Dreaming of a day when all your dreams are simply your daily routines.

Made in the USA
Columbia, SC
19 February 2018